The Tiger Princess

The first book in the Saderia Series

Sarah Renée

First Edition

Tiger Print Books
Mount Pleasant, SC 29466

ISBN-978-0-615-32126-4

Library of Congress Control Number: 2009938305

Printed in the U.S.A.

Dedicated to

My Mom,
A wonderful mother who helped me reach
my dream

~ Contents ~

Chapter One

Princess Saderia

Flames licked up the pine trees, forever scarring their bark and charring them an ugly black color. The leaves were scorched into nothing more than ash as the fire crept violently through the forest. The crackle of flame drowned out the cries of the animals of the forest as they rushed to get water to put out the flames. Trees fell with a sickening crack and smashed against other bushes and trees which then burst into flame. The smoke from the horrible fire turned the normally peaceful, light blue sky into a dark black cloud, choking and damaging the throats of the animals it captured.

The fire spread hungrily from tree to tree without stopping, creating a dangerous ring of flames. The blaze turned the forest red, orange, yellow, and black as forest animals ran for cover while others rushed to put out the fire. Some of the animals yelled as loud as they could and still couldn't be heard over the crackle of flame, the snapping of falling trees, or the screams from the other animals.

The fire was closest to a large den, secluded in one part of the forest. There two tigers were running around screaming orders at anyone they could get to, desperately calling out for two animals.

As a tiny tiger cub, Saderia observed this from safely inside her den. Her amber eyes stretched wide with fascination, wonder and terror as she crawled up to one of the windows to look out of her den and see her forest burning around her. The heat reached her even through the house and she felt fear well up in her small body as she stared out with a quiet whimper. On the verge of tears, she watched the forest and the two tigers that had run from the house closely.

"Karenisha!" one of the tigers who had run from the house screamed.

"Cia, have you found them?" yelled the other one, racing around, trying to find an opening in the ring of fire.

"No!" Cia screamed. "Jash, where are they?!" She raced around the fire, coughing and trying desperately to see through the smoke and flames. "Makero!" she yelled in vain against the deafening sounds of the fire.

They continued to scurry around the forest, yelling for the two missing animals while other animals hurried forward with water. It was almost impossible to stop the flame but no one ever gave up trying. Screams from the fleeing animals floated around in the air.

"Where are the King and Queen?!" someone screamed.

"Where did the fire come from?!" shouted another.

More yells and cries came but were drowned

out by the enraged roar of the fire as it devoured yet more of their precious forest.

Baby Saderia observed all this with huge eyes and a shaking, tiny body. Two fat tears teetered precariously on her eyelids and then spilled over her face, quickly at first and then slowly until they plopped onto the window sill she was sitting on.

"Mommy…" she whispered. "Daddy…"

Saderia's eyes blinked open and she sat up quickly, nearly falling over the edge of her bed. She awkwardly caught herself with her claws and pulled herself up on the bed, clutching her uncomfortable blanket to her chest with her paws. Her breathing came fast as she gasped and panted for air.

Looking around at her feminine room, her horrible nightmare started to drift away as she realized that that was all it was. She was back in her room, safe and sound. And miserable. She reminded herself that she was now ten years old and none of that was happening now.

She stopped gasping and let out a long sigh, blinking back tears. She knew her awful nightmare had been much more than that, rather it was a memory she could never bury no matter how hard she tried.

She slowly relaxed her grip on her scratchy, purple blanket, leaned back against her too-stuffed matching pillows and gazed around at her royal purple room. The rest of her bed was made using different tree branches, stacked together with a thick mattress attached to it. The logs were tinted an elegant deep brown color and the canopy above it was purple with light streaks of pink. Gingerly she pushed the fabric away and stepped out of her bed. She checked the time on the clock atop her re-fined, deep brown bedside table and saw that it was almost time to get up anyway. She definitely was not going to risk sleeping again.

Walking across the thick purple carpet, she made it to the vanity made of sticks and logs on the opposite side of her room, knowing what she had to do but hating it no less. Being a Princess, she was expected to act sophisticated and fancy, when what she really wanted to do was ditch the cosmetics and the 'typical Princess' act and go out to be rough and wild and have fun. But Cia would never approve, and unfortunately she had to listen to her.

She hastily combed through her orange and black striped fur that was now sticking up in clumps from the way she must have tossed and turned last night. Hurriedly she put bows on her ears and smoothed out her unusually fluffy tail. Then she looked glumly in the mirror; she had seen the face staring sadly back at her many times but she knew it was not her.

She barely looked at the rest of her room, with its deep purple walls and the large drawer against the wall where she kept her homework and other documents in. She just stalked out of the room,

4

pushing her horrific dream out of her mind. It always hurt too much to ever think about that tragic time, even though she had been a tiny baby of only a few months old.

Walking out of her room, she started down the hallway, moving past the bathroom close to her room and out into the front room, which was large, with wood floors and elegant wallpaper lining the walls of the den. There was a wooden desk in the corner, two computers on one wall and lots of drawers filled with papers. The desk was slightly uneven, the computers rare and imperfect but they were the best that could be obtained. Saderia's family's rich and royal status guaranteed them the finest things in the forest.

She ignored the hallway opposite hers for fear that it might bring pain after the dream. Instead she turned right into the carefully carved archway that led to the kitchen and dining room where her Aunt Cia and Uncle Jash were waiting. There was another arch at the back of the dining room that led to the living room with wooden, fabric-draped couches and bookcases made from two thick tree branches with little twigs held together to form shelves.

The two adult tigers were sitting at the solid gold table in the middle of the small dining room which broke off into the kitchen. Only sparkling, very precisely made, golden railing separated the two rooms. Watching her aunt and uncle, Saderia quickly went to sit in her place at the table, the chair being wide enough to seat her with her front paws and back paws together in a sitting position. Cia had already made food and left it on the table for the three of them but Cia and Uncle Jash had hardly touched their food. Instead, they were bent over several sheets of paper.

Cia looked up from the paper with troubled blue eyes. The frown on her already worried looking face deepened as she took in Saderia's expression. "What's wrong?" she asked.

"I just had a nightmare," Saderia muttered. She wondered why they both looked so worried. She knew that Cia did worry, mostly about Saderia and her less than Princess-like tendencies, but she usually kept a light, carefree expression to hide that. Uncle Jash normally didn't look so serious either.

Her uncle looked up then, too. "What about?" he asked.

She met both of their blue gazes then looked away. "The fire."

Cia flinched and Uncle Jash looked down.

When Cia spoke again her voice was calm but strained. "Saderia, it's been ten years since that happened and you were just a cub then. Why would you have a nightmare about that?"

She shrugged. "I don't know; I have no control over my dreams."

Cia sighed. "We should have never told you what happened if it gives you nightmares."

"Well, you did and I'm glad you did. I should get to know how my parents died."

Again Cia flinched; Saderia felt guilty about using such harsh words but she couldn't take them back now and her dream had really disturbed her. Another thing that frightened her about it was that Cia hadn't told her in detail what had happened and yet she could picture the scene almost perfectly, although she had witnessed it when she was only a few months old.

Cia shot Uncle Jash a look, clearly asking him to say something to her, so he turned to Saderia and, speaking calmly, said, "Cia's right. Your parents have been gone for a long time, and you didn't even know them since you were so young."

Saderia raised her eyebrows but said nothing. She *had* known her parents no matter what anybody said, despite the fact of her young age. But she didn't try to tell Cia that she knew her mother just as well as Cia knew her sister despite her short time with her. Instead, she decided to change the subject.

"So what's with the paper?" she asked, leaning forward with her paws on the table.

"Get your paws off the table. It's not good manners and your manners need to be perfect if you're going to be a Princess," Cia said automatically.

Saderia sighed but sat back up straighter. She wanted to tell Cia that it wasn't as if she had any choice about being a Princess, being born into it the way she was. But she had learned a long time ago that it was best she kept most of her thoughts to herself.

"So what *is* that paper?" Saderia pressed.

Cia's frown deepened. Looking worried again she muttered to Uncle Jash, "I really wish my sister were here to handle this. She knew how to be Queen much better than me." Saderia guessed she wasn't supposed to hear that so she kept her face composed as she waited for an answer.

Cia turned toward her and put the papers on the table. "Problems. Many animals of the forest have had some very bad luck. Some animals have lost family members." She added more quietly, "Some suspect...murder."

"So they've turned to the King and Queen for help," Uncle Jash finished.

Saderia didn't try to point out that they were *not* King and Queen even if Cia had been born into the royal family and Uncle Jash had married into it. Her parents had always been King and Queen and Cia and Uncle Jash were just taking over the responsibilities until Saderia was old enough to be Queen in ten more years.

"Anything I can help with?" Saderia asked. "It sounds like something a Princess should be prepared to handle when she becomes a Queen."

Cia shook her head. "No, you need to work on being proper and elegant," she said primly, giving her a hard look. "You can learn more about this when you're much older."

How much older? This seemed a much better thing for her to be preparing for as a Princess than learning about where to place her fork or do up her fur. But, of course, it was not part of her training to be a Princess, and the training she got was the kind she hated. It seemed pointless to worry about such insignificant 'Princess' things when she would much rather be out helping the forest animals, solving problems, and making the forest a safer and kinder place.

"Fine," she muttered.

"And, of course, you still have your learning," Uncle Jash pointed out awkwardly.

"Yes," Cia agreed. "And you already have such a hard time with that, so you can't be bothered to do much harder things like this."

Great, she thought. But she supposed it had to catch up with her somehow. She resented Cia and Uncle Jash knowing about who she really was since they so rarely let her be that tiger and also because they were not her parents, so she tried to keep as much of herself and her life as secret as possible. She was really quite intelligent but her aunt and uncle rarely noticed or cared so she just acted dumbly, so as not to expect anything different.

"Speaking of learning, your tutors will be here soon," Cia told her. "We'll worry about this problem; you just worry about learning how to be a proper Princess."

"Great," she said out loud, allowing just a pinch of sarcasm into her voice but not enough for them to give her stern looks.

She looked at the paper and started to wonder if it would be worth it to snatch it when they weren't looking. Then she could get more information and maybe think of some way to help. It probably wasn't worth it but she kept her eyes on it just in case.

Suddenly there was a loud knock on the door of their den, and Uncle Jash hastily took the papers away while Cia and Saderia hopped down from their chairs to answer the door. She knew it would be the tutors Cia had hired to teach Saderia instead of letting her go to normal school like she wanted.

"Why can't I just go to normal school?" she hissed quickly but hopelessly to Cia as they moved swiftly to the door.

"We've had this conversation," Cia sighed in exasperation. "You're a Princess and shouldn't be around the common animals. You have to learn to be sophisticated like a Princess and not ordinary like the other non-royalty animals. You have to be above the common animals."

"Fine," Saderia said. To her, the words 'sophisticated' and 'Princess' meant 'alone' and 'miserable.' It was kind of ironic to her that she was a Princess who was supposed to have so much power and yet no one listened to a word that came out of her mouth. And, of course, she resented that almost as much as she resented the fact that her parents were not there to raise her themselves. Somehow she knew they would listen to her, unlike her aunt and uncle.

When Cia opened the door, three animals stood outside. Two were lionesses although one of them looked sweeter while the other had a sharp, more pointed face and stricter look. Behind them was a pretty, but serious looking black panther.

"Come in," Cia greeted Saderia's tutors and they stepped in. As usual, the three of them curtsied, as all animals were required to do in the presence of royalty, before they came inside. Cia gave Saderia a look and Saderia led them over to the desk and tables in one corner of the front room, reserved for where Saderia's schooling took place.

"We'll be in our room," Cia sniffed as she went to join Uncle Jash and probably look over those papers more.

Saderia led the tutors over to the table and sat down at her desk as they took out papers from their bags.

"We'll begin with math and science," the sharper looking lioness said in a way that seemed almost challenging.

"Okay, Ms. Grenyl," she replied automatically.

With a stern look, the tutor began her lessons for the day. Saderia was used to the way she didn't describe anything adequately enough for anyone to understand. She did, but that was because she had already learned these things on her own, using whatever was available.

"I don't get it," she muttered when Ms. Grenyl had finished speaking. She was completely bored out of her mind, her head drooping over her desk which was covered by a mess of papers.

Ms. Grenyl hissed in annoyance and assigned a bunch of homework to make her get it, but then the panther snapped at her. "Sit up straight, young lady. A Princess *does not* slouch!"

Feeling more and more ruffled, Saderia sat up straighter. "Sorry, Ms. Celen. Better?"

"Speak fluently. Use complete sentences," she snapped.

Saderia took a deep breath, used to the strictness of the tutor hired to teach her useless 'Princess' skills. Speaking clearly and articulately were big things she had to master, but she wondered why they were trying to teach her that when no one listened even when she did speak the way they told her.

"I apologize to you, Ms. Celen," Saderia pronounced each word very carefully. "Is this way that I am sitting better than before?"

"Yes, it is," she said, satisfied.

Increasingly annoyed, but not wanting to misbehave too badly, she was forced to stay very still as Ms. Grenyl continued her lesson.

When she was finished the softer lioness took her place. "Oh, you look so cute with your bows!" she gushed. "Are you ready for your lesson?"

"About?" When Ms. Celen looked at her sharply she rephrased, "What is the lesson about, Miss Lila?"

"Compound sentences," she replied, still mooning over her 'cuteness.' Saderia suddenly felt the urge to throw up at the way Ms. Lila was staring at her like she was a basket of buttercups and daisies.

Saderia suddenly wondered why her tutor was allowed to use short, not complete sentences when she wasn't.

"And other types of sentences," she added, pulling gently at her bows.

Again, that was technically not a sentence but again, she didn't comment.

"I'm as ready as I'll ever be."

Ms. Celen gave her another sharp look since she didn't particularly like contractions but Saderia didn't feel like correcting herself. Ms. Grenyl didn't like her to be sarcastic so she too gave her a hard look but she ignored both of them and started to drown out Ms. Lila as she started talking. When she was finished and Saderia had looked at her blankly, she too assigned a lot of homework to supposedly help her understand.

It was Ms. Celen's turn to teach her about being a proper Princess and Saderia groaned inwardly. The rest of the time she stared off into space with a blank expression, trying to keep herself entertained through the boring lecture of how to speak right, how to eat properly, walk elegantly, and how to look sophisticated.

At the end, Saderia said, "What? I don't understand any of that at all!"

She wasn't lying because, although she understood how to do what the tutor was saying, she couldn't wrap her mind around why any of it was important.

To her, it was demeaning because it took away her personality and turned her into some boring clone of every other royal animal. She liked to think that she was unique in personality and attitude but these tasks the tutor asked her to do were destroying the last pieces of herself that she had managed to hang on to. There was only one thing Saderia was afraid of and that was becoming the stereotypical Princess and losing her personality.

Ms. Celen let out an aggravated growl and snapped, "I do not know how to better explain it! You will just have to practice it to learn it!" She checked the time. "It is time for me to go now, Princess Saderia." She and the other tutors curtsied again and left the room as Cia stepped out to join Saderia.

"Honestly, Saderia, would it kill you to pay attention to what they're saying?" she scolded her, shaking her head. "I was listening, and it's obvious that you don't care enough to try."

"Hey, you're catching on," Saderia muttered with a sarcastic grin, before she got out of the desk, grabbed the homework she had been assigned and started to her room to work on it.

Cia stared after her with narrowed eyes but

didn't say anything as she disappeared down the hallway and shut the door to her room, using all of her self-control not to slam it.

"I hate this!" Saderia shouted, ripping the bows out of her fur when she was in the privacy of her own room. She fluffed up her tail to her liking, feeling the fur along her back start to bristle. Her glare scorched all sides of her room, yet she longed to curl up in it and lay there forever. She rolled her eyes at herself. "I can't believe I have mixed emotions about my *room*!"

Part of her hated this room because of the girly, Princess-y way it was designed, yet another reminder of what she was supposed to be but didn't want to be. But another part of her loved this room because she could have some privacy in it. It was the only place she could be herself because she was alone, and she wished for that every day.

She let out a long breath before going over to her bed to curl up under her stiff, uncomfortable blanket and begin her homework. However, her focus was not on her homework, and she lay there thinking of how the only thing she wanted more than to be herself was her parents. In her mind, she imagined scenes with them and how they would treat her much differently from how she was treated now. She would actually have a voice with them and she could actually be herself with them.

But that was impossible. Her parents were dead and never coming back.

She thought about herself then. The cold shell she showed other animals and what she was becoming inside was not the real her and it upset her to think that she was becoming bitter because of the way she was forced to keep her real self hidden.

Thinking about these things always hurt and she would do anything to distract herself from it. That was why she loved doing the hours worth of homework that her tutors assigned her. It took her mind off of her longing to be herself, for a better life and for her parents most of all. Most animals thought she was selfish and horrible for thinking her life was hard because she was a Princess, who was expected to lead a charmed life. But being a Princess meant nothing to her if it meant she could never express herself.

After several hours of nothing but homework problems, and writing out in perfect, complete sentences the proper things a Princess was supposed to do for Ms. Celen, she put the homework away in her homework drawer. After cramming the overflowing drawer shut, she went to her bed and opened the little drawer in her bedside table to take out the book she had been reading. Reading was very easy and natural to her and it took her to another time, another place, another world. Which was good because she liked anything that distracted her from the charade she was supposed to call her life and the ever-present longing for her parents.

What really irked her was that on top of the annoying 'proper Princess' situation, she was expected to be happy like a Princess should be. Well, the other animals didn't know that she liked to play outside and, yes, get dirty doing it, to do rough things like climb trees and swim through lakes, to help the other animals. They had no idea that she longed to go to normal school, and actually make a friend. Part of her was afraid to express who she really was, for fear of the rejection and scorn which would surely come. And so she curled into a ball and clamped her mouth shut over her tirade of hurt and angry feelings.

But she was bordering on painful territory so she quickly buried her face in her book and tried to ignore the jumble of emotions that wanted so desperately to get out. Slowly she relaxed into the words on the page and read for hours until it got dark. But when she put the book away she moaned as it all came back to her in one painful rush.

"I have no life, do I?" she muttered to the purple canopy over her bed.

The emotions she was feeling were confusing. She usually felt miserable and upset, but these feelings rarely came to her so strongly. Now they were practically all she could think about, and she couldn't help wondering if they had been triggered by the dream. Groaning, she knew that the dream probably had caused these long-buried emotions to return and they wouldn't fade for a long time. That was going to be painful.

She glanced at the clock and noticed that it was almost an hour before she was supposed to go to bed. Opening the drawer again, she pushed the book aside to reveal a stack of clean white paper. She took out a piece of paper and a pencil and began to write. She didn't know why she had to do this, but she always felt the need to.

Pencil gripped tightly, it moved across the paper swiftly, making graceful letters across the page. The only thing elegant about her was her writing and she was actually proud of that; it always made her smile to see it.

She wrote:

Today was another horrible, boring day. Your sister acted just the way she always does. I appreciate Cia. But she's just...Well, Uncle Jash and I just try to listen and get through it. I wish you were here. Then I could be myself. Would you know me? I'm kind, and helpful, smart. I'm someone with ideas and a voice. I still remember you, I think. And the disaster. If you're there, if you can see this or hear me, please Mom and Dad, don't leave me here alone.

She gently put the paper under her pillow, before she laid her head down on it. She knew that in the morning she would dip it in water to smudge the writing and throw it away, but it made her feel comforted during the night, knowing she had not lost her parents, hoping that they could see her. It kept her going.

After a few moments, Cia called, "Saderia, time for bed!"

Saderia flipped the light switch beside her bed to off with her fluffy tail and the room went dark. Cia and Uncle Jash came in a moment later to say goodnight and she said goodnight to them, too. Then they shut the door behind them and their paw steps faded away into the distance.

When Saderia was sure they were in their room, she leapt gracefully out of bed, leaving the light off, and took her book back out. She flipped to the place where she had left off and continued reading. This was another habit of hers. At nine-thirty, when her aunt and uncle expected her to sleep, she wasn't the least bit tired. Her amber eyes immediately adjusted to the darkness and she was able to read without the use of any light.

Saderia liked the dark, and she wasn't afraid of it. It was a nice cover in case she wanted to sneak around, and it was secretive. Kind of like herself. So she had no problem staying awake in pitch blackness alone for a while. She loved being alone.

When she was finished reading at ten-thirty, she curled up under her scratchy blanket and closed her eyes. She waited impatiently for sleep to take her for a long time until she sat up with a frustrated hiss. Not even feeling tired, she knew she wasn't going to be able to get to sleep. Bored and desperate for another distraction of any kind, she threw off her blanket and pushed through the fabric canopy. Padding out of her room she began to walk around to find something to do that might make her tired. She certainly wasn't going to just lie in bed all night because that left way too much time for thinking painful thoughts.

Absentmindedly, she walked out of her room and down the hallway, passing the bathroom again. She stepped out into the dark front room then made her way across to the hallway opposite hers that led to Cia and Uncle Jash's room and her parents' old room. Why she stopped in front of the door that led to her parents' old room, she didn't know and could only credit it to her yearning to have her parents back.

She gently brushed her paw along the height of the dark brown door and her paw stopped at a place that looked as if something had faded away. She knew instantly that something strange was happening but did not react and stood completely still as she stared at the door. But then she was staring *through* the door, and not to what lay on the other side but to another time period from ten years ago.

She pulled her paw back slightly, not sure what to feel, but it was like she was in a trance. Drawing back, she saw that the door was different. The wood was lighter colored and a small red heart shape was painted on the door with a crown adorning the top of it.

Saderia carefully placed her paw back where it had been but instead of feeling the hard wood beneath her paw pad, her paw brushed right through the wood. Everything around her seemed to disappear as suddenly the scene inside the room became clearer.

Her paw dropped down steadily and smoothly brushed the floor to join her other paws in a sitting position. An outside observer, she stared at the scene in wonder and fascination. The blurriness along the sides faded away and suddenly she was staring at two tigers, one lying on the bed and the other one watching the first carefully.

The larger male tiger beside the bed was staring at the female tiger intently, concern darkening his green eyes. The female tiger on the bed with amber eyes very much like Saderia's own seemed happy but at the same time it was obvious she was struggling not to cry out in pain. Saderia realized with a jolt that she was giving birth.

The tiger's body convulsed one time and she fell back on her pillow with a sigh of relief. The cub had been born. The father promptly took the newborn baby tiger and cleaned her up before gently wrapping her in a blanket. Very carefully, he lifted the tiny tiger by the scruff and handed the bundle to the mother who cradled it gently.

The father stroked the newborn tiger's short, yellow orange fur. It had no stripes yet, but they could already see that it would have an unusually fluffy tail, much like the mother. Suddenly the father spoke with a warm, gentle voice.

"What should we name her?" he asked the mother softly.

The mother smiled up at him and snuggled her newborn baby closer. In a voice softened with love, she told him, "Saderia."

The father climbed into the bed beside the mother and her baby and the two of them snuggled and played with their beloved newborn tiger cub. The mother kissed her forehead and then her father did. They both told Baby Saderia they loved her and she smiled back and laughed. Baby Saderia never cried; she had her parents, so why would she? The loving family stayed together until the scene started to blur and then disappeared quickly before Saderia's eyes.

Saderia blinked and found herself staring at the door that led to her parents' room. Only this was the door she had originally come to and the crowned heart her mother had painted had faded and gone.

Chapter Two

Royal Pains

Saderia had no idea what had just happened but a wave of sadness was threatening to drown her. Tears pricked her eyes. Blinking them away, she continued to stare at the door. After what seemed like forever but was really only a few short minutes, she very hesitantly slid the door open a crack. She peeked through the crevice and noticed nothing unusual about her parents' old room. She pushed the door the rest of the way open and stepped inside, closing it behind her. It didn't make a sound and she blinked to readjust her eyes to the blackness of the abandoned room.

She easily recognized the bed she had seen from her vision on one side of the room, but it had noticeable differences. The mattress, blankets and pillow had all been a beautiful, deep cerulean blue but were now faded into a light blue that was almost white. The bed was made way too neatly, showing how unused it was. The light wood from the scene she had seen had now turned the same old, dark color of the door leading into the room. Where there had been another pretty crowned heart on the headboard, there was nothing but a faded smudge where a remnant of her parents' life had once been.

There was a bedside table on one side of the bed. The top was cleared off, and the whole room seemed too clean, making it seem as if it had never been used. It hadn't been used in ten years, but the thought still made Saderia frown sorrowfully.

There was a huge dark brown file cabinet against one wall, probably overflowing with royal proclamations and documents a King and Queen would have had. When she went over and opened one drawer to peek inside, she discovered that she was right and shut it again, not wanting to disturb anything inside. The old door leading into their closet was on the left wall and Saderia decided to peek inside it later.

She moved glidingly over to her parents' old bedside table. Pulling first gently on the knob then harder when it didn't open, it reluctantly slid out, having not been used in ten years. Saderia examined the contents inside. There were a few sheets of paper like in her room, a few pens, two pictures, a little black case, and a book.

Using one paw, Saderia took out the book first and blew the dust off of it. It had a small folded paper bookmark sticking halfway out of it and she guessed that her mother must have been reading it...but had never finished. Saderia had read the story she now held in her paws and considered it one of her favorites. Swallowing the choked feeling in the back of her throat, she placed the book back where she had put it and next pulled out the little black case and the two pictures.

The black case had a piece of paper taped to the bottom and Saderia turned it over to read what was written. Her eyes widened when she recognized handwriting almost exactly like her own on the bottom. It read:

My Favorite Wedding Present!

Saderia realized with surprise that it must have been her mother's writing. She felt sad and happy at the same time to realize that she and her mother shared even more than just their amber eyes and fluffy tails. She glanced at the pictures and her eyes widened when she realized she was looking at a picture of her parents at their wedding. She had thought she remembered the way her parents had looked and her vision had made her believe even more strongly but she was still surprised to find that she had gotten their appearance exactly right in her mind. The picture confirmed that.

Her parents were standing under a large arch with various flowers, each a different shade of blue. Her father had a kind face and was larger than her mother but only slightly. In the picture, his green eyes were bright with happiness. They matched her mother's shining amber eyes. Her mother had a sweet, but excited looking face with a slight wildness to it, much like her own. Like Saderia, she had a fluffy tail that was sticking straight up with excitement. Their faces, bodies and tails were both covered in pitch black stripes; they both looked magnificent and regal.

The other picture was of her mother's face. Her amber eyes were bright and she was wearing a crown with a sapphire jewel on her head, tipped slightly to the side. Besides the crown she was also wearing a necklace with a heart-shaped diamond on the end of it. When Saderia looked closely at the picture, she could make out words engraved on the diamond that said, 'I love you.'

Saderia realized tenderly that her father must have given it to her mother. Next she looked at the little black case and guessed that it might be inside. She gently put the pictures back where she had found them and opened the black case. The inside was silky and covered with black, shiny satin. There was an indent on the bottom where the neck-lace would have gone but there was no necklace. Letting out a sad sigh she closed the case again softly. Almost everything that had had anything to do with her parents had disappeared along with them, it seemed. The desolate feeling she always carried returned.

She put the case back disappointedly and was about to shut the drawer when something bright blue caught her eye. Looking back at the drawer she lifted the paper and the other things out of the way so she could see what was at the bottom. Care-fully she lifted the object she had found and let the other items fall back in the drawer with a quick motion that caused the dust to float up, then settle again.

Saderia blew the dust off this book as well and revealed its brilliant blue color. It was a book with many pages, bearing a lock concealing its contents, one that required a key. She made out her mother's name on the front of the book even though it was faded and hard to read. Then with a gasp she realized what this book was: a diary.

Her mother's diary! Saderia held the book now with shaking paws and stared at it with a slightly opened mouth. In front of her was a possible record of her mother's life, a link she had always longed to have with her parents, at least one of them. She recalled asking Cia for any insight to her parents when she was younger and hadn't known any better, but Cia would never tell her anything. That she couldn't get to know her parent's any better, or at least see if she did know them accurately was a constant torture.

Uncle Jash had been slightly more helpful, but not much. He had told her a bit more about them than Cia had but Saderia's aunt usually told him it was better if Saderia were left in the dark. She believed it would hurt her and when she though Saderia wasn't listening, she told Uncle Jash to stop telling her things. Cia had been wrong because, although it would have been a little sad to hear about her parents when she knew all too well how their story ended, it also would have helped her somehow, in a way she could never describe well. It was like she felt better that she was keeping their memory and proving to herself that she knew and loved her parents, and had a reason to miss them. But she could never quite tell Cia or Uncle Jash that, and gave up trying.

It was then that she fully took in the lock on the diary and quickly grabbed it, unsheathing one of her claws to try to force it open. But then she stopped and sheathed her claw again. She didn't want to destroy her mother's diary. Gingerly, she set the diary on top of the table then ran around the room searching for the key. She checked under the pillows on the bed, looked underneath it, searched for any little hole she wasn't seeing that could possibly hide it, ran over to the file cabinet and began digging through the drawers for it. When she couldn't find it, she let out a frustrated hiss and began tidying the room back up now that it was in disarray. She left it slightly messy looking just so it looked like someone had lived there and felt a little better when she looked around. But she still hadn't found the key to the diary and was getting very discouraged.

She padded over to the closet and opened the door to a very dark room. She set the diary down and walked into the closet, not daring to turn on the light. Her amber eyes pierced through the blackness and she was able to see tables lining the perimeter of the closet with square things perched on top of them. She guessed that they must be picture frames but she couldn't make out what they portrayed. However, a swift search of the tables revealed nothing. Frowning dejectedly, she shut the door quietly behind her when she walked back into the bedroom.

Frustrated, Saderia grabbed the diary and stared intently at the keyhole, trying to figure out what the key would look like according to the notches. She had an idea but that didn't help since she hadn't found any keys at all. Briefly she considered asking Cia or Uncle Jash if they knew where it was, but almost immediately her mind rejected the idea. She couldn't risk them taking away her newly found keepsake because of the pain they thought it might cause her. Their heart was probably in the right place, but she would hate them for it. Some part of her mind knew that she needed her mother's diary, now that she found it, to help her.

Grabbing the diary, she raced out of the room after shutting the door quietly behind her. She bolted through the house until she was safely under the blanket in her own room, clutching the diary. It was then that a strange pang seared her. She had never needed anything to get her through but now that she had found this remnant of her mother, she felt as though she had always needed it but had just never known. Very carefully, she put the diary in the drawer of her own bedside table and then settled down in her bed to wait for sleep. After a long moment of insomnia, she took the diary back out, clutched it to her chest under the blanket, reminded herself of the paper under her pillow as well, and soon enough she had drifted off into sleep.

Her dreams were very strange that night. She thought she heard the clanging and jangling of keys banging into one another and there was an unclear image of her house in the background. Suddenly a paper floated out of one of the windows as if riding a breeze, and when it flashed upward, Saderia realized that it was one of the papers Cia and Uncle Jash had been looking so intently at. Four words jumped out at her: *unknown, treachery, murder* and *parents*... But then the paper that was still floating through the air disappeared into a swirl of ashes that spiraled down to the earth below.

Saderia watched in horror as the ashes fell through smoke into a forest devastated with fire. The fire formed an awful ring beside her house. Suddenly the house was on fire, too, and she watched in agony as the flames licked up and down the house, destroying the outside as well as the inside, devouring tables, couches, beds and anything in its way. By the time the flames had run its course, the whole house was burnt down, leaving only a pile of items behind. Saderia couldn't make out the other items in her dream but among the small pile of items that remained from the horrible disaster she saw a cerulean colored book and a ring of keys...

Saderia bolted awake from her dream, still

clutching her mother's diary to her white chest. She was gasping from the horror of the nightmare dream but the first thought that flew to her mind was that she had to get those papers Cia and Uncle Jash had looked at. She blinked her eyes and slowly relaxed her grip on the diary. Feeling grateful she hadn't damaged it with her claws she carefully put the diary away in the drawer.

Her thoughts instantly flew back to her dream, resulting in a rush of sadness but mainly confusion and uncertainty. The dream hadn't felt like any ordinary dream she had ever had, and in a way, it felt like it was almost trying to tell her something. But that was ridiculous, she decided, because dreams were just dreams. Nonetheless, when she remembered the keys in her dream, she couldn't help but get excited. She knew she definitely needed to check out those papers, and *soon*.

She was just beginning to make a plan for how to find and get the papers when Cia's voice broke through her concentration. "Saderia, something important is happening today! Make yourself look decent and come out here! Make sure to put your tiara on!"

Saderia raised her eyebrows, her thoughts becoming useless vapors, but didn't try to argue. Instead she reluctantly went to her vanity and began going through her normal ritual of 'making herself decent.' When she had gone through the normal stuff, she dug out her royal Princess tiara with a purple amethyst jewel in it; Saderia would have preferred a cerulean jewel, but she hadn't had a say in the matter. She didn't know what was so special now that she would be forced to do this but she had learned that arguing with Cia usually got her nowhere. It was much easier to just do things behind her back.

When she was finished, she scowled at the mirror, hating the way it showed someone completely opposite of who she was. Whatever Cia had planned, it probably wasn't pleasant, but she would have to do it and she would have to fake her happiness. She practiced a quick, fake smile in the mirror that anyone would fall for as long as they didn't look at her joyless eyes.

Without another glance at the fake Saderia, she ran out of the room and out into the front room where her aunt and uncle were waiting, both looking very formal. Uncle Jash looked awkward as usual around formalness, but Cia fit into the role well.

"What's going on?" Saderia asked.

"We're *all* going to a royal party and meeting to talk with our advisors about the situation."

"The one on the papers," Uncle Jash added.

Cia nodded agreement and Saderia nodded along with her, cringing on the inside. She absolutely despised having to go to those royal party/meetings, because they were just royal pains. Since Cia and Uncle Jash weren't technically King and Queen, even if Cia was in the royal family, they needed royal advisors to back them on decisions and listen to their suggestions. Advisors were just some animals in the forest that the current King and Queen elect to help them make decisions. Cia had explained to her that all new Kings and Queens had had them, including her parents, but when the Kings and Queens got more used to their roles, they were no longer needed. Theirs were always needed because the forest always needed some incentive to trust their decisions.

In theory, the meetings weren't a bad idea, and Saderia would have actually liked to go to them to try to work out troubling situations with the others. But it didn't exactly work that way. For one thing, to her the advisors were all nothing but stuck-up, unintelligent animals who just agreed with whatever Cia or Uncle Jash said. For another thing, she never actually got to participate in the decision-making even though she had good ideas; she was just expected to hang around and look like a pretty, good little Princess girl. Ugh.

Saderia sucked in a breath, let it out silently and plastered a sickly sweet smile on her face. "That's a great idea! I can't wait!" she lied.

Cia smiled encouragingly. "That's the spirit," she said. "You're becoming more of a Princess every day."

Saderia decided to take that as a compliment and just kept smiling. Again thinking about her Princess situation, she wondered why Princesses were taught to be so pathetic and helpless when they were supposed to be ruling the forest, but she wasn't going to go into that again.

"We're leaving after we eat breakfast. Remember to use the manners your tutors taught you," Cia told her.

"Yes, Miss Cia, I will," she recited, bored.

Cia beamed. "That's very fancy, Saderia. You're giving the others the right impression of yourself."

Wrong, she thought mutinously, still smiling. It was started to hurt her face. But at least she was making Cia happy.

Cia and Uncle Jash led her into the dining room where their food was already waiting for them. Saderia and Uncle Jash sat down while Cia flitted about in the kitchen, calling, "Do you want anything to drink on the way there?"

"Anything is fine, thanks," said Uncle Jash. "Same here," Saderia added, "thanks."

Cia poked her head out of the kitchen. "How about just water?"

"Fine," Saderia said.

When she disappeared back into the kitchen, Uncle Jash hissed to her, "Boring."

She grinned and nodded as Cia came back into the room.

"I have to go back to my room," she announced. "You two stay here and finish your food."

Saderia and Uncle Jash smiled big smiles and bobbed their heads up and down. Cia left the room, leaving them smiling those huge smiles.

"This hurts my face," Saderia muttered across the table when she was gone.

"I feel your pain," Uncle Jash muttered back.

They relaxed their faces and stared down at the cereal.

"I don't want to go," Saderia murmured, playing with her spoon.

"Neither do I," he admitted. "It would be better if we had better advisors."

"Ones that don't get drunk all the time," Saderia agreed.

"Exactly."

"A fun park wouldn't hurt either," she suggested playfully.

He laughed. "That's true."

Just then Cia walked back into the room with a purple purse hung around her neck, swinging past her white chest. They immediately quieted, gulping down their cereal quickly. When they finished, they got up and waited for Cia to tell them what to do since she was in charge.

"We're going now," she told them. "It's at the usual place. Saderia, you'll be expected to mingle with the advisors and be on your best behavior. Jash, I've got the papers, and we'll go in to discuss them around noon."

Saderia got up from her seat and followed Cia and Uncle Jash out of the dining room, and then to the door in the front room. Cia and Uncle Jash walked out and started out through the forest without a problem, but Saderia hesitated at the door, unsure of going outside.

Cia turned around, looking annoyed. "Don't try to skip this meeting, Saderia. You have to come."

"I...I wasn't," Saderia stammered. "I'm coming."

Gingerly she stepped outside, letting the door swing shut behind her. She was relieved when she felt the cool, fresh air greet her, and when she heard the light, carefree sounds of birdsong. The entire forest looked lush and green, very welcoming and familiar, instead of the fire-devastated, burnt wasteland she had been afraid of stepping into. As she stepped out onto the trodden-down dirt path that led away from her house and into the town, she cast a glance back at her house.

The huge den looked very natural, situated among the trees with holes carved into it for windows, glass added to it later. The pine trees rose up around it, seeming to shelter it from danger, but Saderia could all too easily imagine those same trees bursting into flame and toppling onto her house. She shivered and shook the images out of her mind as she bounded along the dirt path to catch up with Cia and Uncle Jash.

The path sloped off on either side into the wooded part of the forest. No trees blocked their way on the path and sunlight shimmered down on them from above, unbroken by a canopy of trees, unlike in the woods on either side of the path. Cia and Uncle Jash led her far along the dirt path until they veered right and took a rougher path for a long time. Suddenly the trees fell away in a clearing when they reached the end of that path and a big building rose up among the trees. The doors were open and the wind carried over to them voices from inside as well as the smell of food.

"Come on," Cia urged. "Some of the advisors are already here."

With a shared, quiet groan, Saderia and Uncle Jash followed Cia over to the doors leading into the royal building. As Cia was about to push through the doors eagerly, there was a rustling in the bushes behind them and they all turned around as a cool voice called, "Cia. Jash."

Saderia walked a few steps away from the doors with her aunt and uncle to see who had called them. The bushes continued to rustle and a moment later, a dark brown lion with a pitch black mane and amber eyes stepped easily out of the bushes and walked over to join them.

Saderia noticed Cia's ears prick in surprise and Uncle Jash blinked in equal shock.

"Dastarius?" Cia asked as the lion stepped over to her.

The lion dipped his head to her. "Queen Cia."

Saderia flicked her own ears in surprise when she realized that her aunt actually looked awkward for once in her life. Cia uncomfortably nodded back but then stared at the lion blankly and curiously.

"What are you doing here?" Cia asked him bluntly.

"I heard you were having a meeting with your advisors," he told her. "If you remember, I used to be an advisor for King Makero and Queen Karenisha."

"One of their most trusted," Cia agreed, nodding. "Yes, I remember you from my sister and her husband's meetings before…" She trailed off, casting a look at Saderia and then flicking her eyes back at the lion.

Dastarius's eyes flicked over to her as well and he looked at her curiously. "And this is…?"

"Princess Saderia," Uncle Jash told him. "Karenisha and Makero's daughter."

Dastarius's eyes widened in surprise. "So *this* is their daughter."

"Yes, she was just a few months old when…" Again, Cia trailed off.

Dastarius nodded solemnly. "The disaster, of course. It is still such a great loss." He looked at Saderia intently. "I can see the resemblance now. In her tail and eyes."

"Yes," Cia agreed. She continued to study him curiously. "So what exactly are you doing back here?"

"I came to act as one of your advisors again," he told her seriously.

Cia's eyes widened. "Really? After what happened…?"

"Water under the bridge." Dastarius waved

whatever she was talking about away with his black-tufted tail. "May I be an advisor again, or not?"

"Well, we could use your experience, I guess…" Cia looked indecisive but then nodded at him with a surer expression. "Yes, we'd appreciate your help back on the council. Your support would definitely make things easier."

"Excellent. Until the meeting, I hope you enjoy your party." Dastarius walked smoothly past them and into the building, but Saderia swore he was keeping his eyes on her the whole time.

A weird feeling in her gut spread over her, as if warning her of something, but Saderia shook off the feeling, sure she was imagining things. Maybe it was because of her strange dreams. Ignoring it, she followed Cia and Uncle Jash into the building. She noticed Dastarius sliding through the crowd of animal advisors who all gave him curious, if not alarmed and awkward looks. He answered all of their questions vaguely without looking at hardly any of them, making his way through the building undaunted.

The way everyone was staring at him so awkwardly and uneasily made Saderia wonder about what Cia had said to him before. She had hinted that something had happened, possibly to make him quit being an advisor.

Once Cia had gone off into the throng of animals, Saderia turned to Uncle Jash. "Who's that

Dastarius guy?" she asked him.

"He was one of your parents' advisors," Uncle Jash told her. "One of their most trusted and dependable ones, too. He usually had the best ideas and so they viewed him pretty highly."

"But Cia hinted that something happened...?" Saderia pressed.

Uncle Jash sighed. "Yes, something happened. That's why we were so surprised he came back. At one of these meetings, your parents humiliated him in front of the rest of the animals. They didn't do it on purpose but he left and didn't show up for a while, though he said he would still be an advisor. Everyone felt a little awkward then and he didn't return. And then, well, the disaster happened, and he still didn't show up."

"Oh," she said, casting a glance in Dastarius's direction. He was talking to one of the animals who didn't look as unnerved as the rest.

"That incident also caused his mate to leave, supposedly," Cia added, coming up. "She might as well know," she added defensively to their surprised looks that she was actually telling them something.

"Actually, he should probably be grateful for that," Uncle Jash put in.

Cia gave him a hard look and Uncle Jash shrugged sheepishly. "From what I heard of her, she wasn't exactly easy to like. I'm just saying," he defended himself.

Cia rolled her eyes. "Well, regardless, it wasn't

a pretty scene. Don't say anything about it," she warned her.

"I won't," Saderia promised.

"Good," Cia said sternly. "Now, enjoy the party until the meeting starts. And remember, when the meeting is in session, you wait out here until we're finished."

"Okay," Saderia said with a muted sigh, silently berating herself for not bringing a book to read in the meantime.

Cia and Uncle Jash walked away, leaving her alone in the party to mingle with whoever she was forced to. She walked around, talking to lions, cheetahs, panthers and tigers, knowing the names of some while the others were unknown to her. Most of them weren't meant to be advisors, Saderia thought, because they hardly knew what they were doing.

She had retreated to a corner after talking with most of them and was trying to think of something interesting to do to keep her mind free from tedium when a voice interrupted her thoughts.

"Greetings, Princess."

Saderia looked up at the voice and saw Dastarius padding toward her. She began to get that weird feeling about him again and instantly blurted out the first thing that came to her mind, being too preoccupied by the strange uncomfortable feeling to hold it back. "Just Saderia will do," she told him then regretted it as soon as it was out.

He flicked his ears. "So the life of a Princess doesn't suit you." His voice was smooth and collected, somehow intimidating.

"Not the way Cia does it." She blinked and silently cursed herself. Why wasn't she watching what she said? What was her deal? She shook her head to try to get it to function properly because it was unwise to go around blurting out her real thoughts. Even more reckless to do so to this weird lion who she had an incredibly uncomfortable feeling about.

Dastarius raised his eyebrows. "I see you've inherited more from your mother than just her physical traits."

Saderia's ears pricked up instantly. "What do you mean by that?"

He shrugged. "I never knew two animals that fought more than Queen Karenisha and Queen Cia, is all."

The weird feeling she had been getting about him disappeared instantly to be replaced by intrigue. She walked over to him with her ears pricked in interest. "What else can you tell me about her?" she asked, without thinking *again*. She thought furiously to herself that she could have at least phrased it a little less obviously, so he wouldn't know just how clueless about her own parents she was. She almost hissed out loud in annoyance.

Dastarius seemed to be considering her question. "Queen Cia never told you anything?" he finally asked.

"No," Saderia blurted out, closing her eyes to try to assuage her fury at herself. It quickly disappeared to be replaced by burning curiosity and a desperate need to know about her parents.

Dastarius shrugged. "I can tell you that Karenisha was never afraid to let her opinions be known, to put it lightly. She was slightly wilder and rougher than the typical royalty."

"Wow," Saderia murmured, grateful for just these little bits of information about her mother. Mentally adding *opinionated, possibly stubborn, wild* and *possibly playful* to the short list of what she had learned about her mother, she asked, "And her leadership?"

"It was okay. She was intelligent, altruistic, that sort of thing."

She added that and said, "And my father?"

"Makero was a strong leader. He had good ideas, too, but was nice and Karenisha usually came up with the plans and solutions and such." He was staring at her with an unreadable expression but she hardly noticed. She was too happy about the little information she had gathered about her parents to notice anything weird, including the uncomfortable, cautionary feeling that had left her the second he'd started talking about her parents.

"Thanks," she said. "It's really good to finally hear something about my parents."

Dastarius nodded, keeping his amber eyes locked on her face intently. Then his lips twitched in the beginnings of a smile and he said, "So Cia and Jash have you acting like a typical good Princess?"

Saderia was furious to see amusement in his eyes. "It's not funny!"

"I suppose it isn't for you."

"It's not!"

He nodded, serious again. "So, if you're not the typical Princess they want you to be, who are you then?"

Saderia opened her mouth to say something but warning bells went off in her head and she clamped her jaws shut. What was she thinking? She couldn't tell him or *anybody* who she really was, and yet she had been about to. But she knew for a fact that she couldn't do that, that it would be very bad.

"I don't know what you're talking about," she said instead. "I'm a perfect Princess!" She stalked away then, sticking her nose up in the air for good measure, and then ran away more briskly when he was out of sight, blocked from her view by a group of animals.

She went to another corner and immediately started to wonder what had happened to her and why she had just blurted out whatever had come to mind. She hadn't done anything like that with any of the other animals and should know better. She *did* know better, and yet she had acted like an idiot. Why couldn't she remember to keep her thoughts to herself when talking to him? The uneasy feeling returned, baffling and even frightening her for a moment as she puzzled over what it might mean. But she shook it off, fury at herself covering up everything else.

She didn't have too long to brood about it though, because Cia's voice cut through her thoughts like a blade. "The meeting is to begin now. Our advisors need to meet with us in the meeting room now."

Saderia stayed put, knowing with burning frustration that she wasn't allowed to come. Out of the corner of her eye, she looked around to try to see where Dastarius was and what he was doing. She spotted him talking to Cia, and gesturing to her with his tail. Cia looked her way and then back at him uncertainly. Consumed by curiosity, Saderia casually stepped forward to try to hear what they were talking about.

"She's a Princess," Dastarius was saying in a voice that was almost contemptuous. "Shouldn't she come to the meeting to get skills for when she's Queen?"

"Maybe…" Cia said, glancing at the door she had just come from, which led to the meeting room. Dastarius's persuasive tone must have changed her mind because she lifted her head and called, "Saderia, you're allowed to come to the meeting!"

Saderia pricked her ears and blinked in surprise as she walked forward in a way that was clearly automatic. She hadn't expected that at all but that didn't mean she wasn't excited. "Thanks," she said to Cia and Dastarius as she passed by them. Her tone of voice was thick with surprise and almost disbelief but neither of them noticed.

Inside the spacious meeting room there was an extravagantly long table with two large chairs at the end of it and rows of chairs all along the sides for the advisors to sit in. The two broad chairs at the end were clearly for her aunt and uncle, the Queen and King at the time. Uncle Jash was already sitting at one of them. He raised his eyebrows when he saw her walk in and look around, uncertain of what she should do.

Saderia looked up as Uncle Jash walked over to her where she was standing at a corner in the room while the advisors all took their seats.

"What are you doing here?" he asked her quietly.

She shrugged. "Cia said I could come."

"Um…okay…" He looked like he didn't believe her but then Cia walked in with Dastarius dragging two chairs over to the other end of the table. When she didn't say anything even when she clearly saw Saderia, Uncle Jash decided not to question anymore.

"We sit down there," Cia explained when she came over. She flicked her tail toward the two big chairs on the end of the table. "You can sit…" She seemed to consider it for a minute.

"I'm sitting here," Dastarius spoke up, nodding to one of the chairs he had pushed up to the other end of the table. "She can sit there." He indicated the chair next to it.

Cia nodded her agreement. "Good idea."

Although uneasy about it, Saderia went to sit next to Dastarius without another word while Cia and Uncle Jash went over to sit in their big chairs. Ignoring the prickling of her fur at being so close to this strange lion, she began forming a rough plan in her mind of how she would act. She couldn't blow this opportunity and needed to show her aunt and uncle that she was responsible enough for these kinds of tasks suitable for a Queen. She decided not to say anything for a good portion of the meeting until she completely understood what was going on and had listened to the comments of the others. Then she would think *very carefully* before she said anything, and it had to sound intelligent, like she knew what she was doing.

Cia started the meeting by saying, "I'm sure all of you know by now that we have a situation involving possible homicide and kidnapping. I'm going to start out by passing around the papers detailing what exactly happened, and then I want you to give your opinions on what you think it is we're dealing with and then what we should do about it."

Saderia felt a jolt of excitement that she would get to see the papers but that brought a flashback of her dream and again she felt addled and scared. She remembered the words, thinking to look for them on the paper when it came around to her.

Cia took out her purple purse and retrieved the papers from inside it, passing it around to the left side of the table first. A few animals shared it, trying to get the gist of it before passing it on to the next group of animals. When it finally came around to their side, Saderia and Dastarius both leaned over the paper to study it closely. She couldn't help but glance uneasily at Dastarius, who was staring down intently, before she devoted her full attention to the papers.

Saderia silently sucked in a breath when the words from her dream jumped out at her from the paper. The paper was detailing the loss of family members for some animals and the sentences the words belonged in varied. The word *unknown* was in several sentences about the cause of the sudden disappearances of some animals. The word *treachery* was written in a report of what the animals suspected had happened, that maybe their family had turned on itself. The word *murder* was definitely not a rare occurrence on the page as it detailed what the supposed cause for the loss of the animals' family members was. The word *parents* was only written once in a sentence that described what the animals who had lost children, the parents, thought had happened.

Forcing herself not to react, she passed the papers on when she and Dastarius had finished reading over it. The rest of the animals glanced at it and then returned the papers to Cia. After that the discussions began, and the majority of them agreed with the cause of the losses being murder, while few disagreed. Some speculated about who could have done it but most of the discussion was dedicated to how they would find that out.

Saderia thought very thoroughly about what she should say and finally decided on saying, "We could probably talk to the animals who have lost family and figure out the last place they were seen. It might be smart to try to figure out if the place has something to do with them or something to tie them in to the supposed killer. We could also try to find out if the ones that were killed had anything in common, or something like that."

At the same time Dastarius said, "We should see if there was someone most of the families knew that could have done this. We should check their families' alibis and start forest-wide searches. And yes, the Princess took the words right out of my mouth--her suggestions are wise."

While Saderia suppressed her surprise, feeling a brief glow of happiness at how he'd praised her, Cia said to him, "You may have a point. We'll find them and speak to them as soon as possible. Saderia, your suggestion was good, too." She sounded surprised and Saderia raised her head a little higher with pride. "We will also try to organize as many searches as possible."

A few of the other animals spoke up throughout the meeting and Cia and Uncle Jash acknowledged their suggestions. Saderia added a few small details, but through the meeting she was sure she felt Dastarius's eyes on her. She didn't look in his direction and kept her thoughts on the meeting but couldn't help the creepy feeling that sent shivers along her spine and raised the fur along her back.

Cia eventually ended the meeting and the advisors started back to their homes. Cia and Uncle Jash led Saderia out after the rest of them and they turned toward the path that would take them home. Dastarius was the last to exit the building after them.

"We appreciate you coming to the meeting," Cia told him.

He flicked his tail. "Anytime. I expect I'll be hearing about anything new you find out."

"Yes, you will. Maybe we should meet tomorrow after we've collected any new information."

"I'll be there. Until then, Queen Cia, King Jash." Dastarius dipped his head and looked at Saderia. A slight smirk that she was sure no one else saw crossed his lips. "Princess Saderia." Then he turned around and walked off into the bushes.

Saderia scowled after him but Cia and Uncle Jash were already leading her back along the path to her house.

When they reached their house it was in the afternoon and Saderia hurriedly retreated to her room to read or preoccupy her mind. But when she opened the drawer in her bedside table to take out her book, she saw her mother's diary first and a terrible longing to know who her mother had been coursed through her again. She gently took the diary and stared at its cerulean cover for a long time, as if trying to see *through* it like she had with the door of her parents' room. After half an hour of staring at it, she thought she caught a faint glimpse of an amber-eyed tiger running through trees, her fluffy tail streaming behind her in the blue depths of the book, but the second she saw it, it was gone. She hissed in furious frustration that she had lost it.

Saderia looked at the lock on the diary again and, with a terrible ache, *knew* that she had to find the key. She desperately needed the key to her mother's past.

Chapter Three

The Ring of Keys

After just a few moments of pondering where she could find the key, Cia's voice calling her name broke through her thoughts.

"What is it?" Saderia called back, putting up the diary.

She heard the sounds of paw steps walking down the hall to her room and a moment later Cia stepped through her door.

Saderia blinked and raised her eyebrows. "Come in," she said, gesturing broadly with her paw.

Disregarding the sarcasm, Cia said, "Saderia, we're going out into the town to talk to some of those animals, like we discussed at the meeting. Are you going to be okay staying here alone?"

"Yes," Saderia exclaimed, too quickly and enthusiastically. "I mean, uh, sure, I'll be okay."

Cia frowned at her but said, "We'll be back soon. Be good."

"I will."

Saderia watched as Cia walked back out, shutting the door behind her. She felt giddy at the thought of being alone, as she always did. It felt good to have the whole house to herself. Then she smiled at another thought. She did have the entire house to herself while Cia and Uncle Jash were gone, and that gave her a great opportunity to search for the key to her mother's diary.

Flipping the blanket up over her with her fluffy tail, she pretended to read casually until they were gone. Her eyes couldn't make sense of the words beneath her and she read a sentence several times without understanding a word of it while she listened for the sound of her aunt and uncle's departure. Finally she heard the sound of the door shutting in the front room along with the turn of the key in the lock. She laid the book aside gently, but had no guilty conscience about throwing the blanket away and practically ripping the canopy over her bed in her haste to start rummaging through the house.

As the door shut behind her she froze and looked down the hall, wondering where to begin the search. Her mind instantly began running through the layout of the house and she tried to think like her mother, not a hard thing to do, to find the key's hiding place. She couldn't quite picture where it could possibly be hidden in any of the rooms, especially since it had been ten years or more since her mother had hidden it, but then a new thought came to her. Her mother and Cia were sisters, so it seemed logical that Cia might have the key after the disaster.

She darted down the hall, crossing the short distance in the front room to the hallway opposite hers. When she stopped outside the door to her aunt and uncle's room, she felt a brief flash of guilt that she was going to raid their room, especially since she knew how precious privacy was. But she pushed the thought away, her own need for knowledge about her mother driving her forward.

She pushed through the door and went over to the bedside table, seeing it first. She dug through Cia-ish things like fancy accessories and jewelry, along with a few pictures and other things but there was no key. There was a vanity on Cia's side and she even checked that but no sign of the key there either. There was an elegant deep brown file cabinet made of cut tree logs and she looked in it as well. Nothing. Next was a tiny dresser where Cia kept all her many formal accessories that Saderia thought looked absurd, but that didn't matter because there was still no key.

Finally she went to the closet, it being her last hope in the room. She opened the door and automatically flipped on the lights using her tail. Looking around, she saw a table with a pile of pictures on it and a bunch of stuff that must have been from Cia's childhood. On another table there were two crowns but she barely looked at them. She went over to a big basket with flowers and other things that lit up the room as a beautiful display and read the card that was attached to it.

Sorry, Sis. Yeah, I forgive you for being a jerk sometimes (just sometimes?) and we're friends, of course. Sorry about that fight. Yes, I'm apologizing and, yes, I mean it, but if you tell anyone about this, you are going to be in big trouble. Love, Sis.

Saderia blinked, recognizing her mother's handwriting and guessing she had written to Cia. She smiled slowly; it proved that her mother and Cia had been close. She noticed a card laying beside it with one of the flowers from the basket taped to it. When she opened the card she recognized Cia's handwriting, similar to her mother's and her own, and realized that she must have written this card back to her mother, but must have found it later…after the disaster.

Apology accepted, Sis. We're definitely still friends even though you can be a jerk sometimes (try always) but we're sisters so what can I say? The fight's forgotten. And I won't tell anyone…for now. Love, Sis.

It was at that moment that Saderia realized Cia must miss her sister as much as Saderia missed her mother. Guilt seared through her, making her fur prickle, guilt that she had thought so badly of them for not understanding her own grieving. She had been overly concerned with her own feelings and had never considered how Cia must have felt. Shame stung her throat for raiding her room now but she knew she might as well finish what she had started and search the rest of the room.

As she looked around the presents and pictures of Cia and her mother growing up together, she tried not to think too much about how badly she thought of herself now. When she hadn't found anything and gave up to stand at the back of the closet with a resigned sigh, she finally let the thoughts sink in. With a fierce stab of pain, she realized how desperate she was, and that made her feel very low. She also knew that she was greedy, selfish and insensitive which were all blows to her mental image of herself as well. She was beginning to think that maybe she didn't know herself too well. Maybe she had lost track of herself somewhere along the line, or maybe she had just been like that to begin with. She didn't like to think that she had been wrong but there was no getting around the fact that she was. For a long time, she had thought Cia was the one who was wrong for treating her the way she did but when Saderia treated her just as unfairly, that clearly made her a hypocrite.

She had broken into Cia's room, gone through all of her things, hated her for treating her badly when she was no better, insulted her, and Cia hadn't done even half of that. She hated feeling so guilty and dishonorable but she couldn't deny that she hadn't been the least bit kind or understanding to her aunt. Cia had taken in a hateful brat and tried her best to raise her and that was what Saderia repaid her with.

Saderia groaned, furious and horrified at what she had done, and leaned back heavily against the wall but jumped back with a startled cry when her side crashed into a hard bump in the wall. Frowning, she turned around to see what she had hit her head on. At first she was confused when she didn't see anything at all but when she looked at the wall more closely, her eyes widened in wonder as she made out a brown lump protruding from the wall. It almost looked like…a handle.

Blinking, she tried to sift through the thoughts that crowded her mind at that realization. Since it had been so hard to see, it almost seemed as if it was supposed to be hidden, and for a reason. Was there some sort of secret here?

Cautiously, Saderia extended one paw and gripped the handle, pulling it toward her. The handle pulled a section of the wall with it and opened up a tiny compartment in the wall with hinges to move it easily. A *secret* compartment! The wood of the secret compartment was lighter but all Saderia could see inside it was an old newspaper, so she couldn't see why it was so special as to be kept in a place so secret.

She pulled the newspaper out of the secret compartment and looked at the front page. There was a big red circle around the headline but when Saderia read it, she instantly felt her body go numb and cold.

Worst Fire In History

Saderia looked past the headline and began to

read the article. The second she read the first line out loud to herself, she immediately felt sick and coldness gripped her body and her heart. Though it tortured her, she couldn't help but read on in a hoarse whisper.

November 17th, 1996, the day the worst fire in history devastated the forest. The fire took place mostly in the west area of the forest and struck near the house of the King and Queen. The fire spread quickly and much of the forest was burnt down.

The fire seemed to form a wall just outside the house, coming very close to it. The house stood but unfortunately, King Makero and Queen Karenisha were lost. It seemed that they ran out to try to stop the fire but the wall of flames separated them from the house. The smoke was thick so they could have choked on the smoke, and then because the fire was so quick, it could have destroyed what remained. No bodies were recovered.

The details are highly unclear and no one knows exactly how the fire was started.

Saderia threw the paper down on the ground, wanting to shred it. *Why* had Cia kept *that* in her closet? She could sort of understand why it would be hidden in a secret compartment now, but why had she kept it at all?

As she forced herself to calm down, she realized that maybe Cia had reread it to try to see if there were any way her sister and brother-in-law were still alive. She studied it more closely and realized it had said that no bodies had actually been found but could have been burned away in the flames. She felt a shiver of horror as she had the thought and pushed it from her mind. She guessed that it must have given Cia hope and she had kept it for that reason, but it had been ten years now so there could be no more hope.

Taking a calming breath, she picked the newspaper back up to put it away so that Cia didn't know she had been there. But when she turned back toward the secret compartment to conceal it again, she stopped when she saw what *else* was hidden in the secret compartment.

A ring of three keys.

The newspaper fell from Saderia's paws as she grabbed for the keys. The jangling sound they made as she yanked them from the compartment reminded her briefly of her dream but that thought flew away the second she held them in front of her face with a shaking paw. Disbelief, relief and then happiness surrounded her as she realized she must have finally found the keys she had been looking for. At that, she forgot all about how guilty she had felt about breaking into the room. It had been worth it.

But as soon as she had had that thought she was seized by confusion as she watched the three keys sway from the ring she held clutched in her paw. One of those keys must go to the lock on her mother's diary, but what were the other two for?

Sarah Renée

Were there more secret compartments around the house, ones that required keys? Then she had a darker thought as she realized that if there were, Cia and Uncle Jash had kept that from her. But why would they do that?

She didn't care if they had lied to her, once she really thought about it. They kept a lot of things secret from her but she had other means of finding out. Right then all she cared about was getting back to her room and opening the diary to learn its secrets.

Without thinking, she grabbed the newspaper and crammed it back into the secret compartment, no longer caring about what it said. She closed the compartment and then ran out of the closet, slamming the door behind her. Dashing out of the room, she didn't stop to think about making it look like she hadn't been there. Hopefully it wouldn't matter because she had been careful at first to put everything back where she'd found it.

Knowing the way around her house by heart, she didn't have to stop to think about where to go. She automatically ran for her room, as she had been doing for so many years, and slammed the door shut behind her. She was used to running for her safe haven, but now she had another, happier reason for it, and she threw the canopy curtain aside before jumping onto her bed and snatching her mother's diary from the drawer.

Eagerly but carefully, she tried to stick the first key in the lock but it wouldn't fit so she let that one drop. She managed to stick the next one in the lock but she couldn't twist it to unlock it, so she yanked that one out and let it fall too. With a smile, she reached for the next key and put it in the lock, knowing that one had to be it. But when she tried to twist it to unlock it, the smile fell right off her face to be replaced by a frown and a growing sense of frustration and disappointment. She yanked it out and tried all of the keys all over again but the lock never clicked open and the diary remained as mysterious as ever.

Saderia hissed furiously and threw the ring of keys across the room. She didn't put the diary up as violently, even though she was burning with disappointment and frustration. With a sigh, she realized how irrational she was being and went to pick the keys up. As before, with the keys in her paws she felt a tug of curiosity and her dream flashed through her mind for one brief moment. She went back to her bed and this time pulled the canopy down to cover the entire bed. She even pulled it over the end of her bed, even though she usually kept that part open so she could see her room. At that moment she wanted her privacy.

Studying the keys for a very long time, she began to think back to her dream without consciously deciding to do it, almost as if she wasn't in control of her own mind. She doubted it meant anything as it was just a bizarre dream from her overactive imagination. But she did remember the diary sitting with a pile of keys on a table in the middle of a burning house. It had seemed in her dream that they were the only things left from the violent fire, and so maybe they were clues as to how to get information about her parents. It being the only thing left was just coincidence in her strange dream, but at least it had given her a hint as to what to think of the ring of keys. That seemed right, but she explained her dream as not having meant anything because her mind had simply known that she treasured the diary and needed the keys to it, and so it had come up with that picture.

She decided that there must be more secret places in the house that she had never known about, places that had been kept secret from her. Suddenly she felt as if she didn't know anything anymore and, remembering how she had felt when she realized how wrong she was in Cia's closet, she realized she probably didn't even know herself. She buried her face in her pillow, her mind whirling and upset.

As a natural response for whenever she was feeling this way, she started murmuring to her parents, allowing it to calm her horrified panic. Automatically, she tried to convince herself that she still knew herself, focusing on anything good she could come up with.

"I'm kind, I'm dependable, I'm..."

She trailed off and looked up from the pillow at nothing in particular. Her eyes drooped with sadness and resignation.

"No. I'm lying to myself."

She looked around her purple enclosure sadly for a moment before sighing and sitting up.

She was lying to herself, she wasn't any of those things and she knew it. She hadn't exactly shown anything to prove otherwise. What she was was just a shell of what she could be and what she wanted to be. For a moment, she let herself despair at this fact, knowing that all her efforts to keep her true personality had been worthless. But then she became determined. If she wasn't those things, then maybe she could be if she put her mind to it. She had to figure out just who she was and she had to do it by breaking out of the life of monotony her aunt and uncle had laid out for her.

At the same time, she couldn't disguise the burning curiosity inside her as she thought of her mother's diary and the keys. So she was curious; whether that was good or bad remained to be seen.

It could be a good thing because it could drive her to find out more, but it could be a bad thing if she found out something she didn't want to have found out in the process. But she knew that no matter how much she tried to change her mind, she would be looking out for the diary key, and for a place the ring of keys would unlock. For several heartbeats, her body burned with anxiousness, her chest searing with longing to know the truth.

But before she could go through the house to search once more, she heard the sound of a key in a lock and jumped. For a moment, she was sure she was hearing things in her yearning to find out what to do with the keys, but then she heard the door open and realized it was only Cia and Uncle Jash returning.

Jumping out of bed, after carefully hiding the keys and the diary, she ran out to greet them, anxious to know what had happened and if any light had been shed on the crisis outside of her home.

"Hi, guys," she said when she saw them. "What happened?" She tried to remember that she should be nicer to Cia and Uncle Jash for all that they *had* done and added, "Um…do you want me to get you guys something to drink or a snack or something?"

"Some coffee might be nice," Cia said, giving her a mildly curious look.

"That'll work for me, too," Uncle Jash said, mimicking Cia's gaze.

"Okay." Saderia went running off to the kitchen. Jumping onto her hind legs, she poured them a cup by the time they got into the dining room. Cia had taken out more papers from her purse when Saderia walked in, carrying the coffee. Saderia brought the drinks to both of them then sat in her own chair, trying not to slouch just to show them that she could respect the ways they had taught her. She kept her mouth shut even though she was dying to know what had happened, so as to give them time to relax from their day.

After a while, it became clear they weren't going to tell her on their own and prompted, "Did you find out anything new?"

Cia gave her a look, as if deciding whether or not she should share with her, then looked back at the paper. Nodding she said, "Yes, the supposed murders actually seem more like kidnapping now."

"Well, that's sort of good news because at least there's a chance they're alive, right?"

"Right, and that's what we're hoping for. However, there are no clues as to who took them and why."

She nodded, taking the little information in and looked to them for more. "What are you going to do about it?" She wanted to come up with something to show them that she was smart and ready for more than just helpless-Princess training, but she wanted to be nice, too, and let them keep their authority.

"We're going to track down the places where the kidnapped animals spent the most time and see if there's any clues there, of course. We didn't have time to do that today." Saderia realized that it was already dark and wondered how the time had passed so quickly. But Cia was talking again. "We'll try to find out if there was anyone who had anything against them, to try and determine if there's a common suspect for all of them."

"That sounds smart," Saderia complimented her.

Cia smiled briefly at the praise although she looked a little suspicious at Saderia's sudden change in attitude. She turned to Uncle Jash then. "We should probably talk to Dastarius to see if he has any leads or ideas."

At the mention of Dastarius, all rational thought flew out of her mind and a bad feeling made Saderia's belly churn. Before she could stop herself, she blurted out, "No! You can't!"

Cia and Uncle Jash turned to her at the same time with questioning expressions. They obviously thought she had completely lost it, but they must have decided to humor her because Cia said, "Why do you say that? Why shouldn't we?"

"This is really serious and you shouldn't let any information get out when we're dealing with kidnappers and stuff like that," she blurted before she could think about it. Regretting it the instant she said it, she wished she could just disappear or melt into a puddle of orange and black fur. Why wasn't she able to control herself now? What was wrong with her lately?

Cia looked at her in confusion then narrowed her blue eyes. "Are you saying we shouldn't trust him? He was your parents' *most trusted* advisor and he can always come up with some sort of plan in times like this to help."

Saderia shrunk back against her seat, wishing she could disappear into it. "Okay, I'm sorry. That wasn't what I was implying, I just...I'm just worried, I guess."

She turned back to Cia who started talking again in a lighter tone. "I understand that, and you haven't known him long, I suppose. Nonetheless, I can tell you he is trustworthy and none of this information will leak out to anyone else. We'll talk to him tomorrow."

Ignoring the uncomfortable feeling that gave her, she said nothing this time. Feeling infuriated at herself, she realized she didn't even know why she was so uneasy when Cia and Uncle Jash obviously trusted him. She didn't even know him. She must just be paranoid from the dream or finding the keys and secret compartments.

"You've got a while before you have to go to sleep," Uncle Jash pointed out, changing the subject. "Do you want to do something?" He sounded hopeful but before Saderia could reply, Cia spoke.

Her tone was matter-of-fact and carefully composed when she said, "No, Saderia probably wants to go to her room like any other night."

Saderia bit her lip, feeling guilt wash over her again. Cia and Uncle Jash hadn't done anything horrible to her but she had shut them out all the time. "Actually, I'd like to stay out here with you guys tonight. We could do something fun until bedtime." Even though she longed to retreat to her room, she managed to smile at them.

"Okay..." Cia sounded surprised. "What do you want to do then?"

Saderia shrugged.

Uncle Jash saved her. "We could go to the living room to play a board game or something.

There's not much time for anything else."

"Okay," Saderia agreed quickly. That wouldn't be too hard to get through, and it was an easy thing to start off a hopefully better relationship. Taking it slow might be best.

Following Cia and Uncle Jash out into the living room, she sat down on one of the couches while Uncle Jash got a game. She made the right comments when she needed to, and talked to them occasionally, but still felt guilty that she longed to hide in her room. She just wasn't comfortable with talking to them, or anyone for that matter, especially when she was so clueless as to how to act. At the same time, she felt relieved that she was spending *some* time with her aunt and uncle and even a little happy. She couldn't remember the last time she had spent time with them like this.

When it was time for her to go to sleep, she said goodnight to them politely and started back to her room casually, even though she wanted to run. She *did* like to spend time with them, but she still preferred to be alone in the sanctity of her room. Once she had curled up in her bed she turned the lights out, after her nightly ritual of reading.

Practically the second she closed her eyes she heard the crackle of vindictive flames and the moaning sigh of trees as they fell to the ground with a crash, igniting more flames. Red, orange and yellow blazed up in front of her threateningly but suddenly she could see through the towering wall of fire. The branch of a charred, smoking tree was reaching out, as if trying desperately to escape the cruel, roaring fire. On one of the branches it had snagged a paper, along with a ring of keys swinging on another branch. A cerulean book sat atop the branch, tottering precariously as if it were about to fall at any minute to the taunting flames below.

Again Saderia was able to see four words jump out at her from the paper speared by the branch but one of the words was different. The words were *unknown*, *treachery*, *kidnapped* and *parents*. The branch had pierced the paper in the place where it used to say *murder* and the word *kidnap* was written right above it, untouched by the shaky stick. Saderia reached out to the branch in her dream, trying desperately to find out what it was about, but in an instant the branch snapped and fell into the flames below; she thought she heard it scream. Horrified, Saderia caught a glimpse of a sharp, glinting claw retreating from the scene before the dream began to fade.

She woke with a start and was surprised to see daylight pouring through the window in her room. Blinking to try to clear the morning haze from her mind, she wondered about her dream and blamed it again on the trauma from the fire so long ago. The things she had seen were just objects she had in real life that she longed for. But then she thought back to the claw that must have snapped the branch and an uneasy feeling overcame her, so strong it hurt.

Then she shook herself, frustrated that an insignificant dream had shaken her so badly. Maybe she had mistaken what she'd seen in her dream, or maybe she was just afraid for those animals who were losing family members, since she had been hearing about that. Maybe she was just paranoid or upset about the fire, as usual. Dreams were strange anyway, so why was she even worried about it?

Suddenly Cia's voice floated to her from down the hallway. "Saderia," she called. "Come on, we're going somewhere."

Saderia frowned in confusion, starting to forget her fear as she walked out of her room and down the hall to find her aunt and uncle standing in the front room. "Where are we going?"

"To meet Dastarius and see if he's found anything out about what's going on," Uncle Jash informed her.

Swallowing a pang of unease, she asked incredulously, "And I'm coming, too?"

Cia nodded and gave her an expression that was as close to a smile as she could get. "I think you can probably handle matters like this. It'll be Queen training."

A glow of happiness inside her made her break out into a true smile and she raised her head higher in pride. Her heart had begun to beat fast in disbelief. Were they serious? She almost believed they weren't, but judging by Cia and Uncle Jash's expressions, she could tell they meant it.

"Thanks," she said. "I'd be glad to come."

"Good," Cia said. "I expect you to be on your best behavior."

Ignoring a pang of hostility toward herself, as if annoyed at being annoyed, she followed her aunt and uncle out of the house with her fluffy tail held high. Again they followed the dirt road off into the woods path and ended up at the building they had gone to for the meeting. When they arrived it was deserted except for Dastarius who sat in the middle of the clearing waiting for them.

Saderia hadn't expected to feel so nervous when she saw him and she instinctively took a few steps back. Cia frowned at her but she hardly noticed, keeping her eyes on Dastarius all the time as if he were a snake about to strike. She noticed that his expression was dark and even though they were dealing with serious business, it seemed too dark.

Dastarius walked toward them. "Queen Cia, King Jash," he said formally. Saderia noticed that even though he had been greeting her aunt and uncle, he was keeping his eyes on her and that made her even more on edge. Something about him didn't seem right but she didn't dare mention it.

Wasting no more time with formalities, Dastarius asked, "Have you spoken to some of them?"

"Yes, we have," Cia reported. "Have you?"

He nodded. "What have you found out?"

"Well, it's starting to look more like a kidnapping, instead of murder."

"I agree. I haven't found any evidence leading to who might have done it, however."

"Neither have we," Uncle Jash told him.

"Don't tell him that," Saderia blurted out.

"Saderia!" Cia rounded on her instantly. "What are you doing?" she hissed more quietly. "We've already had this discussion and we can trust him!"

"I'm sorry!" Saderia stammered. "I...I didn't mean..."

"It's okay," Dastarius said smoothly. "This is serious business after all. It's never a bad thing to be too careful." Saderia swore his tone turned cruel and mocking as he added, "And I can understand why she, or any of you, would be upset since we're talking about the loss of family members."

Saderia felt her fur start to bristle and she wanted to hiss but she bit down on her lip to keep it from coming out, biting so hard in her panic that she drew blood. Discreetly licking the blood away, she tried to avoid the look Cia was giving her.

Cia let out a soft hiss in her direction. "You should go home now, Saderia," she said quietly.

Saderia felt her ears and tail droop and she looked at Cia with a pleading expression. She wanted to hiss in frustration at herself that she had blown her one chance to show Cia that she could handle more important things.

"Now," Cia growled.

Saderia looked down, averting her poisonous gaze, and started to turn to leave but Dastarius spoke up first.

"There was no harm done," he said. "The Princess should stay."

Saderia almost snapped at him not to call her that but decided that would not be the best thing. Cia, still glaring at her, motioned for her to stay put for a moment.

Cia still looked uncertain but Dastarius said, "Is it not a Queen's job to look after her forest?"

"Just behave for the rest of the time," Cia hissed to her.

"Yes, Cia," Saderia muttered, looking down.

Dastarius seemed almost amused at the hostility between them as he went on. "I've talked to just a few of the animals. There doesn't seem to be any pattern yet. I've checked the places they were last seen as well. There were no leads. I've started a few search parties but I'm beginning to think the kidnapper just takes them at random. "

"That's useful information," Cia agreed. "We haven't had time to talk to them yet but we will as soon as possible. ...But if you're right about the kidnapper, it will be an even worse problem."

Dastarius nodded and passed them a sheet of paper. "These are the places I've already checked. You could look into the other ones to see if they're the same way."

Over Cia's shoulder, Saderia saw that the paper contained *many* names, rather than just a few. It made her somehow uneasy that Dastarius was taking over all of Cia and Uncle Jash's work and leaving them few to check themselves. It was almost as if *he* were telling *them* what to do. However, her aunt and uncle didn't seem to find anything odd and Cia took the paper gratefully, saying, "Thanks, we'll do that soon."

"Well, if there's nothing else to report, I should go."

"We'll come to you again if there's anything new," Cia told him.

"And I'll do the same," he replied, starting to walk away.

For some reason, those words made the fur along Saderia's back rise up, as if they were somehow a threat. But she forced herself to stop being so edgy, and realized that there were much worse things that she'd have to worry about now.

Cia turned to her with a flint-like expression. "Let's go."

Saderia nodded meekly and followed after them with her tail drooping, being careful not to meet their gazes and keep her head down. For a while they moved on without talking but when they were getting closer to the house, Cia hissed, "Saderia, I don't know what got into you, but that was rude and embarrassing."

"I'm sorry--"

Cia interrupted her. "I thought you were ready for tasks like this, but apparently I was wrong."

"I'm sorry!" she exclaimed. "I didn't mean to say that!"

"Well, maybe you should think before you

speak."

"I try to! I've been doing that for practically my whole life! I just...I get a bad feeling around him," she admitted. She knew the second she said it that Cia either wouldn't believe her or wouldn't care.

Cia hissed exasperatedly at her. "That's ridiculous. I've already told you that he is very helpful and trustworthy. Do you have any evidence to prove otherwise?"

Saderia opened her mouth to speak but then shut it again, because the truth was that she *didn't* have any proof against him. He seemed to be all that Cia and Uncle Jash said he was but she couldn't help the feeling she always got when she was around him. But then, what did a feeling prove? Nothing.

"I'm sorry," she said sincerely. "I really didn't mean to be rude and embarrass you. I promise I'll try to...to think before I speak next time." She repeated what Cia had said, and meant it because she was very angry at herself. "I...I know you're probably right about him," she went on, less sincerely in that statement, but continued, "I don't know what came over me. I'm sorry."

"You should be," Cia snapped. She sighed. "Obviously, you're not ready for these tasks."

Saderia's heart sank and she wanted to wail in disappointment but decided that would just prove even more to Cia how unprepared she was. So she sucked in a breath and said in her calmest voice,

"Okay, I understand. I really am sorry."

"Well, I'm glad you know why I'm doing this." They had reached their den and walked inside, locking the door behind them. "We have important things to do. We're going to look over the paper and then go out to see what we can find out. You *cannot* come."

Saderia swallowed. "Okay." She turned around and started for her room as Cia and Uncle Jash started to look over the paper. She saw Uncle Jash give her an apologetic look before she turned around and she returned it with a weak smile, glad that he was at least trying. As she walked down the hallway, careful not to make it so obvious that she wanted to get out of there, she wondered whether she should be happy or sad about not going with them. On one hand, she liked to be alone, but on the other, it meant that they didn't think she was responsible enough for Queenly training, thus she had made no progress at all.

She walked into her room, climbing into her bed and pulling the canopy around it to completely shield her from the rest of the world. As she laid down and pulled the scratchy blanket over her, she wondered why she should have expected anything other than the way Cia and Uncle Jash treated her. She thought back to how wrongly she had reacted when there was no good reason. She barely even knew Dastarius yet she had automatically distrusted him for no good reason. Cia was probably right when she had said Saderia wasn't ready to handle bigger things like that.

The more she thought about it, the more she realized they were probably right about a lot of things. She had found out that she didn't know herself as well as she would have liked to think and yet she had thought her aunt and uncle were unfair. She hadn't done a thing to thank them for what they *had* done, and who was to say that the way they were raising her was wrong? Another thing they were probably right about was that it was wrong to expose her to anything that had to do with her parents. Ever since she'd had the dream about the fire she had been too hopeful and curious.

Hope always made things worse, as far as she was concerned. If she had just ignored and tried to forget about that dream, she wouldn't have set herself up to hope for things that were out of her reach. She had overexcited herself about a diary that would probably hurt her rather than help her if she ever *did* manage to get it open which didn't look too promising. She had also gotten too carried away over the keys she had discovered; they probably didn't lead to any secret rooms because that was just her crazy imagination getting out of hand. And she had had no right to steal Cia's property.

Saderia sighed, knowing that she'd have to go back to her old life now, the monotonous life she had had before she had gotten too involved with the past. The only thing that would be different now would be that she would try a little harder to appreciate her aunt and uncle and act like they thought she should. It was probably the least she could do to repay them. Not to mention the fact that she would work on keeping her thoughts to herself, no matter what any 'feeling' told her. Why had she listened to that 'feeling' anyway?

She took out the book she had been reading and buried her face in it while laying on her white belly. She was trying to drive off the all-too-familiar pain that came from knowing that this boring life would probably never end, because she would never have her parents who would truly understand her.

Later in the day she heard the door to the den being unlocked, opened and shut and knew that Cia and Uncle Jash had returned. She didn't call to them to ask them what had happened and how it had gone and they didn't call to her to give her any updates either. She could already guess they had found what Dastarius had said to be true, which made her doubt herself even more. It was clear that he was trying to help, even if he was sort of a jerk, and so far she hadn't seen one reason to distrust him, as Cia and Uncle Jash had said. And if he had been such a trusted advisor for her parents, it definitely didn't make sense for her not to trust him.

She thought back to the royal meeting and remembered that Dastarius *had* told her a few things about her parents when no one else had. How could she dislike him so much when he had given her part of what she had so strongly hoped for? For that, at least, she should be able to put up with him and quiet the wrong feeling she always got. And besides that, he had stood up for her...in a way, first by telling Cia to let her come to the actual meeting and then by suggesting that she stay even when she had openly stated how she mistrusted him. No one else ever stood up for her.

There was something odd about the way he did things, though. Even when he had been helping her, he hadn't exactly *asked* Cia for anything; he had more or less demanded it, in a subtle way. It was almost as if he thought *he* controlled *them*. Then again, Saderia really shouldn't judge him, especially since she was no better at treating animals fairly. She didn't give him or anything another thought as she pressed her face deeper into the book, only pulling back when the words got too blurred to read.

Much later, she heard Cia's voice calling to her. "Saderia, time for dinner!"

Without any enthusiasm, Saderia pushed the canopy aside, put up her book, and walked stiffly out of her room. In the dining room she sat in her usual spot, feeling like a robot because of how automatic the reaction was. She had missed lunch and was starving, but barely noticed her hunger as she slid into her chair and started gulping down the food Cia had made. She didn't even care what it was she was eating. Everything mostly tasted the same to her now, so it didn't matter.

She walked back to her room feeling just as hungry as before she had eaten. Inside her room, she took out her book and began reading until Cia and Uncle Jash came to say goodnight to her. She almost went directly to sleep instead of staying up late and reading, but decided against it and continued reading the book, trying to get back into the normality of her old life.

When she put the book up and pulled the blanket over her face, her subconscious immediately began dreaming. The dream was short but it seemed to be saying more than it let on. All Saderia could see in her dream was the cerulean book and it remained there for a moment, nothing else happening in her dream. Then she started to see words through the cerulean cover and after a moment she began to see them more clearly.

The words, written in her and her mother's shared handwriting, were very clear in her dream but then seemed to fade into the blue background. In her dream she couldn't yet understand what they said.

She awoke the next morning feeling as confused as ever, but deciding to ignore the dream because it was, after all, just a dream. It didn't matter what it was supposed to be and she had already chosen to forget about the diary. The dream and the more exciting life she had begun to discover were pushed to the back of her mind as she turned her back on her past and looked somberly forward to the gloomy and hurtful future.

Chapter Four

Incentive

It being Monday, Cia soon called to Saderia to tell her to get ready for her tutors who would be there soon. Without giving it a thought, she got up and went to her vanity to prepare for the long day ahead of her.

She sat in her normal spot at the table when she went out to eat breakfast with her aunt and uncle.

"We're mainly going to focus on the kidnapping crisis," Cia reported while they were eating

"Okay," Saderia said without much enthusiasm.

A moment later her tutors showed up and she led them over to the desk where she always did her lessons. When she gave them the homework they asked for they didn't question why the answers were all right when they assumed she was dumb; they just guessed that they had done a good job teaching.

She sat through Ms. Grenyl, Ms. Lila, and Ms. Celen's boring lectures about whatever subject they were on; Saderia didn't even really know since she was paying even less attention than normal. When one of them asked her a question, she didn't answer since she hadn't been listening to hear it.

"Are you listening?" Ms. Celen shouted, slapping the desk with her tail.

Saderia snapped out of her fog with a jolt and blinked as if she had just woken up. "Huh?" she asked dumbly.

Ms. Celen hissed in frustration. "I asked you a question!"

Saderia was silent for a long moment, deep in thought, but when she couldn't think of what the question could possibly be, she sighed and admitted, "I wasn't paying attention. Sorry. Could you repeat the question?"

Ms. Celen hissed and muttered something about her being irresponsible and annoying.

"I thought you said muttering was bad," Saderia couldn't help but point out.

The tutor glared at her but Saderia didn't flinch, even when she said in an icy tone, "That is not something a Princess would do. I'm trying to teach *you*."

"I hear animals learn better if they're given a good example, which I've seen none of," Saderia said just as icily, not sure why she was being cold.

Ms. Celen practically exploded and launched into a tirade about her horrible behavior which Saderia didn't pay attention to, just pretending to listen to her when she was really just staring off into space and wishing for it to be over.

"Do you understand why you've been a horrible Princess?" Ms. Celen finished.

Saderia was quick to reply. "Yes, Ms. Celen! I understand why I've been a horrible Princess completely! It's because I actually have a mind of my own! Is that the correct answer?"

Ms. Celen whipped around in frustration and started for the door. "I'm not teaching you."

"You're supposed to curtsey," Saderia pointed out as she got to the door. "When you leave a Princess's presence, you're supposed to curtsey."

"I refuse," Ms. Celen growled, narrowing her eyes. "You'll be treated like royalty when you act like it."

Saderia smiled. "Okay, Ms. Celen. I really hate it when animals curtsey to me anyway. It makes me feel weird. Have a good day!" She really did hate it when animals bowed to her because it made her feel strange and different than everyone else. Even though she *was* different from them, being a Princess, she still felt uncomfortable with it.

As the tutor stormed outside, she grinned after her, feeling just the tiniest bit bad at making her so angry, but momentarily not worrying about it. She hadn't asked for this anyway.

"Have you been listening to a word any of us have said?" Ms. Grenyl snapped, glaring at her.

Saderia sighed, the adrenaline from the argument wearing off. "I'm sorry," she said sincerely. "But no, I haven't. Give me extra homework or whatever so I can 'get it' and it'll be fine, right?"

"You're not teachable!" she exclaimed. "You're just pigheaded and smart-alecky!"

"I'm sorry."

Ms. Grenyl hissed and handed her a huge stack of books that she assumed was her homework before stalking out. Ms. Lila looked around helplessly, gave her some homework, then left awkwardly, curtseying to her in the way she hated.

Saderia sighed, waiting for Cia to run out of the room and screech at her for being stubborn and mean. Saderia did feel bad because she really hadn't meant to fight with them; it had just happened and she really wished she could take it back now.

Just as she had feared, Cia burst out of her room and raced over to her with an infuriated expression. "Saderia, what have you done?!"

"Apparently I've made a big mistake," Saderia replied glumly, feeling honestly ashamed.

Cia looked a bit taken aback that she had admitted to it but she immediately went back to her enraged state. "How could you have said such things?! That was incredibly rude!"

"I don't know why I said it, and I know it was rude," she replied truthfully. "I didn't mean for it to happen."

Cia let out an exasperated sigh and snapped, "Why weren't you paying attention?"

Saderia longed to tell her the truth that she already knew what they had probably been talking about but then she would give away one of her secrets and didn't feel like cleaning up that mess. "It was just...boring." That sounded like a typical answer so she stuck with it. "Sorry, I got the gist of it.

I'll listen next time."

"'Next time!'" Cia narrowed her eyes at her. "It's always 'next time' with you! What happens when you run out of 'next times?!'"

Saderia flinched at the words, and looked away, unable to say anything.

Cia glared at her a moment longer. "Go to your room!"

Saderia got up slowly from her chair then raced to her room as fast as she could, taking her homework with her. Once inside her sanctuary, her head drooped and she let out a sigh of her own. "Nice," she muttered to herself as she walked over to her bed to begin her homework.

She missed lunch again but barely noticed it, just kept going with whatever she was doing. At dinner, she finally noticed her starvation and walked out to eat with Cia and Uncle Jash. Cia gave her dirty looks which she ignored, wishing she'd get over it already. At the end of dinner Uncle Jash came over to her after Cia had gone.

"Are you okay?" he asked her. "You seem upset today."

She shrugged. "I'm fine."

"Are you sure?"

"As sure as I can be."

He paused. "Well...if you, uh, need anything, you can talk to me," he told her awkwardly.

She looked at him out of the corner of her eye, suddenly longing to tell him how she felt about missing her parents and what kind of life she wanted for herself but pushed that thought out of her mind. Muttering, "Got it. Good to know," she walked out of there and toward her room. "Tell Cia I'm sorry," she tossed over her shoulder as she shut the door behind her, not caring if he heard her or not.

The next day, Saderia got up, quickly made herself 'presentable'--one of Cia's words--and then walked out of her room to gulp down breakfast and wait for her tutors to bring what would probably be a very hard time. She had decided last night that she would try her hardest to pay attention now, no matter how boring it was and greeted her tutors as friendly as possible when they showed up.

"You're acting better," Ms. Grenyl said suspiciously.

With an inward sigh, Saderia said, "Thank you, Ms. Grenyl."

She nodded haltingly and launched into another one of her vague, boring lectures. Saderia tried her hardest to listen to her but still drifted off a few times. It didn't really matter, though, because she was able to answer all of their questions which seemed to satisfy them. Ms. Lila was a little nicer so Saderia told her that she had done a good job teaching her at the end. She had a lot more difficulty with Ms. Celen's questions because she hadn't taught herself Princess etiquette and she usually either forgot or didn't pay attention to what that tutor taught her.

Ms. Celen got mad at her of course, since she hadn't done well in her subject area and Saderia spent the next few minutes deflecting what was verbally thrown at her. Finally Ms. Celen left in a huff, accompanied by the other tutors, and Saderia retreated to her room.

Cia came and knocked on her door a moment later. When Saderia said that she could enter, in a tone as polite as she could muster, she was glad to see that Cia's face was warm and approving.

"You're doing much better, Saderia. I'm glad you're listening and trying now."

Saderia just smiled back, internally grimacing at having to sit through the boring lectures. But she liked to see Cia happy, especially after what her aunt had put up with, and so decided that as long as it pleased her aunt and uncle, she'd try her best to be nice.

The next day passed pretty much the same and Saderia was starting to feel her old boring life taking hold of her again. She tried to be nice to her aunt and uncle and get along with her idiotic tutors like she'd promised herself she would, but could feel herself starting to forget that rule she'd laid down for herself. Soon she found herself just trying to get through the week and the time until she became Queen.

She had had the dream about the diary a few times but could never make out the words. The dream had eventually disappeared altogether when she continued to push it away from her. She somehow got through the rest of the monotonous week and was soon sitting at lunch with her aunt and uncle on Saturday, listening to them talk about the kidnapping situation which they hadn't yet resolved, and trying to force herself not to pay attention.

She did hear when Cia said, "Saderia, we're going to meet up with Dastarius and try to trace some leads we've heard. Will you be all right alone?"

"Sure," she replied, ignoring the feeling that arose, as any other time, when she thought of Dastarius. She forced the feeling to disappear, reminding herself that she had no reason to dislike him.

"We're leaving right now," Cia informed her. "Finish your lunch."

Cia and Uncle Jash left the table a moment later and Saderia finished eating. An impatient feeling in the back of her mind told her that she should be excited that she was alone and take advantage of that aloneness, at least to relieve some of the boredom that clung to her from the week.

She went to her room and started reading a book, trying to ignore that annoying little voice, reminding herself that she'd just be setting herself up for disappointment, but after reading a sentence in the book ten times without understanding it, she gave up and tried to think about what she could do while she had her free time. She still felt sorry for the animals that had lost their family and wanted to help them look for their missing children. It would be a waste of time since she had no idea where they could possibly be, but she still wanted to try to look for them, just to make herself feel like she was helping.

Briefly she wondered how long it would take Cia and Uncle Jash to get home and ascertained that she could dedicate at least an hour to searching without them returning and finding her missing. She put up her book, then opened the window in her room to climb through it easily, not wanting to bother with the door. If Cia and Uncle Jash came home and found it unlocked, they would be suspicious whereas if they didn't, she might have a little extra time to get back before her absence was noticed.

As soon as she was outside, she started running off into the woods behind her house, going right, passing the house, and then just going wherever her paws took her, weaving through the trees and avoiding prickly bushes and vines that grew throughout the woods. It was very easy for her to move about freely in the woods without feeling trapped by the towering canopy of trees overhead. Her feelings came from her having grown up there and her love of exploring the forest when Cia and Uncle Jash had let her on rare occasions.

As she ran, she scanned the forest for any sign of the missing young animals, but doubted she would find anything. She felt a little guilty for enjoying the rush of wind in her fur when she was supposed to be helping, but didn't try to hide her enjoyment at being free. Out there, among the peaceful trees swaying in the wind and the calming chatter of birds, it felt as if everything would be resolved and turn out just fine.

Giving herself to the feeling of freedom and choice, she sped along through the forest agilely, letting herself smile at the exhilaration. She ran through the trees as fast as she could go, moving so quickly that she was far away from her house in a matter of minutes. She kept her eyes level with the horizon line, not needing to look down to avoid tangles of briars, bushes, or thick tree roots. But when her front paw smacked into something incredibly hard, causing a surge of pain to shoot up her leg, she cried out and fell forward, scattering the brush and vines that covered much of the ground in front of her.

Crying out in pain, she eased herself to the ground to look at her throbbing front paw. Once she had nursed her aching paw back to health, enough so that she could stand on it, she thrashed awkwardly about on the unusually thick covering of vines and bushes, trying to find a footing. As she finally managed to stumble to her paws it occurred to her that the ground beneath her was too smooth unlike the bumpier ground she had just been running on.

Glancing down at the place where she was standing, she noticed something gray underneath her paws. Curiosity sunk its claws into her deeply. She quickly began to push the bushes away from the grayness it was hiding, snapping the vines with her teeth and claws to shove them away. When she had cleared enough space to see what was under her, she gasped, feeling her claws dig into the cool, smooth stone beneath her.

Below her was a big gray slate, smoothed across the ground. The way it was positioned made it seem as if it were covering something underground. While her thoughts whirled in wonder, Saderia suddenly started to make out some of the faint lines scratched across the smooth surface. At first glance they appeared random and unimportant but when Saderia looked closer she realized that they meant something and were engraved into the stone for a reason.

With her eyes, she traced a pattern of lines that had been faded by time until she finally realized that they had once formed a drawing of a tiger wearing a crown. Above it, she thought she saw a name inscribed and struggled to read it.

"Qu…een…Ta…rae," Saderia made out, squinting to make sure she had seen it correctly. "Queen Tarae." Her eyes widened as she took in the faded tiger picture. Queen Tarae must have been one of her ancestors because her family was the only royal family she knew of. Then she gulped as she realized that the slate below her must be concealing a tomb for her ancestor because, although she couldn't entirely make out the date below the animals name, she knew it was somewhere in B.C. times.

Scrambling to get off of the slate covering the tomb, Saderia noticed something above the name and stopped, unable to keep her curiosity from getting the better of her. She pushed aside a vine and found herself looking at some sort of coded lock. There were five slots with wooden blocks in them that turned to different pictures. Saderia guessed that there was some sort of code that dictated which order to put the little pictures in, and if that code were correct, it would open the tomb. She flipped one of the wooden slots and saw that there were five pictures: a crown, a heart, an eye, a scepter, and something that looked vaguely like a fluffy cloud.

Saderia stared at the code lock for a long time, wondering if she could figure it out but knowing she couldn't. Nonetheless, standing there made a strange feeling surge through her entire body; it wasn't a fearful feeling but she couldn't quite place it as happiness either. The feeling was indescribable but it felt...uplifting, powerful, and she continued to stare at the little pictures in the code lock.

Then she suddenly remembered why she was out there and how much time she had left, realizing that if she didn't start back now, she wouldn't beat her aunt and uncle home. Quickly covering the slate over the tomb with bushes again, Saderia whipped around to race back home and avoid that disaster.

When she reached her den, she climbed through the window and dove into her bed to pretend like she had been reading the whole time. Sure enough, a few seconds later she heard the door open and shut, announcing her aunt and uncle's arrival. Saderia decided she might as well be polite and walked out of the room to greet them.

"Did you find anything?" she asked.

Cia shook her head, upset. "No, there's still no trace of anything."

"Oh, I'm sorry," Saderia murmured quietly.

Cia sighed and walked down the hall to her room but Uncle Jash lingered a moment.

"Are you all right?" he asked her finally. "I mean, it must be upsetting about what's happening now…"

Saderia nodded. "It is, but I'm all right. You don't have to worry about me."

Uncle Jash nodded and after a moment started awkwardly after Cia but turned around when Saderia called him.

"Uncle Jash, who's my oldest ancestor? On my Mom and Cia's side, I mean."

He thought for a moment then replied, "Queen Tarae, I think. I remember your mother and Cia saying something about it long ago."

"Tarae. Got it. Okay, thanks."

"No problem." He looked like he wanted to question why she had asked but must have decided against it, turning instead to walk down the hall after Cia.

Saderia went over to the computer against one wall in the front room, jumped and settled herself into the chair in a sitting position. She used one claw to push the keys while balancing on her other three paws. Once on the internet she clumsily typed Queen Tarae's name in the search box, deciding she wanted to know more about her ancestor and about that tomb, remembering the strange feeling that had filled her when she had stood there.

She clicked on the first link she saw, one that promised an interesting story about her oldest ancestor, and began to read.

Queen Tarae

Queen Tarae is the oldest ancestor of the forest's royal family that can be traced. She is the first in a long line of royalty starting in early B.C. times. Therefore all of her descendants would be linked to the royal family, including Queen Karenisha, Queen Cia and Princess Saderia, rulers of the forest in the present time. Her original parents can never be known since they both died shortly after her birth.

Saderia sighed, knowing all too well what that

felt like, then continued to read, already feeling connected to her oldest ancestor in a strange way.

She went to live with an abusive uncle. Then he was killed by a plague that also affected Tarae. She fought to get over the plague which she did eventually, with natural medicines. After that, she lived in a dark part of the forest and looked after herself.

Even as an orphan, she was fighting to improve unfairness. She walked among the others and solved disputes as well as caused them, always winning with her genius. She improved society and also healed many animals with the natural cures she discovered in the dark woods where she lived.

But because of her healings and cures, her increasing popularity and vision to end unfairness, some of the animals grew afraid of her and made a plan to destroy her. They tied her to a tree in her forest and set it on fire. She clawed herself out of there, but she was badly burned. She survived that, as well, but now had no home.

One of her grateful patients, an elderly leopardess, took her in and helped raise her. She grew up seemingly depressed and saw the world with a new and different perspective. She saw the injustice, unfairness and violence and she wanted to do something about it.

The fact that she was a presumed threat weighed her down but she fought for her rights and eventually became Queen without meaning too. She merely wanted to help but as Queen she could do so much more and she was a great ruler.

She made great advancements in literature, science and mathematics.

Her nature was very sassy and this was how she was seen. She saw the world, she saw the pain. But she kept her high spirits and used common sense to help many. She grew to earn many animals' respect as well.

But she was also a very solitary, introverted person and kept to herself when she wasn't fighting for improvements. Perhaps because of this she ruled alone, not wanting to marry, for fear that a King would take over her power.

When she grew older she decided to carry on the royal family and married a tiger named Macedoniay. He did not take any of her power and she still did most of the ruling but they had a daughter, Taharah, who continued the line.

Macedoniay died before her but she kept her grief to herself and continued her reign of success. Less than a year later, she died and her daughter, Taharah, succeeded the throne. The causes of Macedoniay's and Tarae's deaths are currently unknown.

Saderia found her story interesting, and that she could sympathize with her oldest ancestor. She found it inspiring how she had managed to get past all the difficulties in her life and still go on to be a great Queen. For a moment, Saderia wondered if she would be able to do that someday.

Then she realized that her life was nothing like her ancestor's and when she became Queen, there would be no dramatics. Until then, she would just have to live the life planned out for her by Cia. She decided to find out more about her ancestor and the weird feeling she had gotten by her tomb, typing in 'Queen Tarae's tomb.' Surprisingly there weren't many articles. But she found one that seemed to know what it was talking about even though it was short.

Queen Tarae's Tomb

Many legends have sprung up surrounding this noble Queen's tomb. No one except the current King or Queen knows exactly where Queen Tarae's tomb is.

The tomb is said to be filled with gold and riches but there is an unspoken law that the riches are to remain in the tomb as a sign of respect. None of the royal family have broken that rule.

There is an old myth that says there is some kind of hidden power in that tomb that belongs to the royal family. Legend says that this power was passed down in the royal family. Nobody knows whether it is true or not.

Saderia blinked when she finished reading it, feeling excitement fill her. There was some type of power hidden down in the tomb? She wondered if her mother had known about that, and if Cia knew it now. Not that she was going to ask her.

She looked again at what it said about the power and wondered if she had inherited the mysterious 'power' or if it sometimes skipped a generation. But she decided with a sigh that she probably didn't have it. She didn't feel powerful or any different from anyone else except that she was royalty.

Still, what she had read had started to inspire her and she went the rest of the day thinking about what had been said in the article, feeling something stir within her at the prospect of such excitement. Cia and Uncle Jash remarked on her happier mood at dinner but she just shrugged and smiled, not knowing quite why she was so happy. Happy wasn't really the right word, but she had nothing else to call it.

After dinner she talked with her aunt and uncle for a while about easy things like homework and what her tutors told her about. Sometimes they talked about a book they had all read and it felt good to try to connect with them. Sometimes she valued a little inspiration in her life, and when it was finally time for her to sleep, she slipped into unconsciousness before reading.

The instant her eyes closed, she was off to another place in a dream she didn't completely understand. But after just a moment it became slightly clearer and she noticed the cerulean book in front of her. It was locked as always, but this time it had a certain *glow* about it, as if it were very important and begging for her attention. She realized subconsciously that this was the dream she had repressed before, and her mind briefly thought about trying to send it away but instead dismissed *that* thought and embraced the dream.

As with her other dreams, the bright cerulean color began to fade into the background as words seemed to burn through the cover. But this time was different; she gasped with surprised joy when she realized that she could read them. The words were:

Trust your intuition.
Never give up.

Saderia stared at the words for a long time in her dream until she was sure she would never forget them, and then they began to fade slowly, then more rapidly until she was waking up from the dream, lying on her belly then sitting up to take in her surroundings.

As the dream flooded her mind, again filling her entirely with those words, she felt the same uplifting feeling she had felt standing over the tomb of her ancestor. It was as if something were burning inside her to do something, even though she didn't know what.

She didn't realize she was grinning, probably moronically, as she leaned over and checked the time on her clock. When she saw what time it was: five in the morning, she didn't want to go back to sleep and knew she wouldn't be able to anyway. Without thinking, her paw slid down to open the drawer on her bedside table, and she took out the cerulean diary that had once belonged to her mother. Frustration and longing flowed quickly through her when she remembered that she had no way of opening it without damaging it; the burning desire to find the key was stronger than ever.

She pushed the diary under her pillow and padded silently over to her door. She opened it carefully, trying not to make a sound, then closed it softly, tiptoeing down the hallway. Her paws whispered across the floor and she was pleased by her stealth as she crossed the front room and made her way over to the hallway that Cia and Uncle Jash's and her parents' old room were on.

Fortunately, her aunt and uncle's room was on the end of the hall so she wouldn't have to sneak past it as she crept into her parents' room. Once inside, she looked around hopelessly at the huge room, knowing the key could be hidden anywhere in there, or not in there at all. Knowing she didn't really have the time to check the entire room thoroughly, she headed for the closet to at least make sure she had completely searched that part.

Closing the closet door behind her, she felt safe to turn on the light, blinking as her amber eyes adjusted to the sudden brightness. When she was able to blink the colors away from her eyes, she looked around the closet to see that white tables lined the room, each with a light blue fabric draped over it neatly. Picture frames stood upright on each table, a gallery of her parents' lives.

Instead of looking for the keys quickly, she went over to the photographs, curious to see what they had captured. Her heart ached but it was a good sort of ache when she saw that they all portrayed her parents. There were pictures of graduations for her mother and father, pictures of them as infants and kids growing up, and of parties they must have gone to.

She went to the back of the closet where there were three tables. The table on the left showed a picture of her mother and father and Cia and Uncle Jash all together with big smiles. The one on the right showed a picture of her mother and father's marriage. But then, turning to the picture in the middle, Saderia's mouth opened as if to gasp but nothing came out. The picture in the middle showed her parents in the background but the main focus was a young tiger cub wrapped up in a blue bundle. The label under it was: Saderia.

Saderia stared at it for a long time, but as she did she began to notice something about the wall behind it. It was different somehow, with light lines indenting the wood almost invisibly, and then there was a slight lump in one part of it. The longer she stared at it, the more she knew that something was definitely strange about it. On closer inspection, she finally realized why it looked so strange.

It was a door.

Chapter Five

The Single Key

Her eyes widening in disbelief, her mind flashed back to the moment when she had discovered the secret compartment in Cia's room. She had wondered if there were more places like that. Could she have been *right*?

Hardly daring to breathe, she hopped back onto her hind paws, letting her front paws fall and hit the wall then pushed on the wall gently at first, then harder when it didn't move. When she saw a slight crack in the wall, she pushed even harder until the door fell away with a soft groan to reveal an old, dusty chamber. Saderia blinked in shock and quickly but carefully pushed the table and picture of herself away so she could get past it and enter the room.

Leaving the door open, she looked around inside the small chamber she had entered. It was dark, the only light being from the illuminated closet behind her. It looked like a place that would be dank and overrun with spider webs and creepy things, but it was actually very comfortable in there. Apart from the cramped space, and a bit of dust, it was very pleasant and clean.

Saderia just barely took any of that in because her gaze was transfixed on the wall directly across from the one she had entered. There was another door right across from her, only this door seemed heavier and there was a big lock on it; she knew she had no hope of picking it with just her little claws.

But even the heavyset, locked door eluded her full attention when she noticed a table standing right next to it. It was a small, wooden table just barely her height, but it was what lay on top of it that grabbed her undivided attention. She gaped incredulously as hope filled her. Forgetting to be afraid or surprised, she rushed toward the table and hovered over the small golden key; it seemed to wink at her when she grasped it in her paw. There was also an album on the table and she looked through it briefly, seeing images of her parents, but deciding to look through it more later, back in her room.

She knew, almost without a doubt, where this key went but she had to make sure it didn't go to the door first. She tried, without luck, to open the door with the golden key but when it wouldn't open, she was unsurprised. Still ecstatic, she grabbed the key and album then raced out of the small chamber, making sure she shut the door behind her tightly. She flicked out the lights on the closet as she bolted from her parents' room, making her way silently but quickly toward her room.

Rushing to her bed, she grabbed her mother's diary out of her drawer, then pulled the canopy over the entire bed to give herself privacy. Any tiredness she might have felt about waking up at

5am were drowned by the wave of excitement coursing through her as she gently pushed the key into the lock. A perfect fit, she turned the key and heard the lock click. She held her breath as she tried to open the diary…and succeeded.

Her joy was replaced by surprise and bewilderment when she turned to the first page in the diary. A page that read:

Karenisha's Diary

There are two rules that I stick by. Both are very important.
Those rules are:
1. Trust your intuition.
2. Never give up.

Saderia's dream came flooding back to her and she could do nothing but stare at the page in shock that the words were the exact same from her dream. As she stared, a sort of excitement and happiness sprouted inside her and she realized that she would finally be able to learn about her mother. No longer caring about the likeness to her dream, she eagerly flipped to the next page to begin reading what her mother had once written.

August 20, 1990

Saderia was further stunned, just by reading the date. That was sixteen years ago. Doing the math in her head, she decided that her mother must have been about sixteen years old.

Today Mom and Dad are going to do some royal speech thingy for the forest. Sounds boring. But anyways, my sister and I have the whole house to ourselves now before school starts again! The only problem is that Cia invited her <u>boyfriend</u> over!

Jash is a nice guy and all but I feel so left out because I don't have a boyfriend. Yet. And Cia usually ignores me when he's around, and when she does talk to me, she's usually rubbing it in my face how <u>she</u> has a boyfriend and <u>I</u> don't, which gets extremely old! Sometimes having a sister is annoying! I'm so sick of her rubbing this stuff in! But I have to go and pretend to hang out with them now.

Be back soon. Hopefully.
Karenisha

The thrill of excitement she felt as she read the page was somehow dimmed by the surrealism of it. It seemed strange to be reading something about her mother's life and her thoughts, especially when she had thought that she would never know what she was like, apart from what she could remember. At the same time, it filled her with sadness, knowing that her mother would die in six years and never know her daughter. Nonetheless, she turned to the next page and began reading again.

A few minutes later
Hey, I'm back! Well, that's over with, although they did let me hang out with them for a while before I became a third wheel. Did I mention I hate that? I do.

But anyway, we hung out for a while and Cia acted okay except for the fact that whenever Jash is around she turns into an ever bigger moron. I sure hope <u>I</u> don't act like that when I get a boyfriend! But finally it was over because Cia said Mom had given her permission to go out somewhere with Jash. Yes, I was jealous and stomped to my room which Cia said was immature but I didn't care.

Cia's such a jerk! Well, and lucky. I want to go out and I should be able to! After all, I am the same exact age as her. Well, older by a few minutes, but who really cares? Oh yeah, we're twins in case I forgot to mention that. (Forgot? Yeah right. More like I wished it weren't true!) (Sometimes.) Anyway, Mom and Dad are going out somewhere else and Cia and Jash are going somewhere so I have the whole house to myself and a really cool thing to do is explore the house.

There are all kinds of secret places around here. Mom and Dad told us that but they said we could explore on our own. I claimed the first secret room I found. There's a door in my room in the closet and it leads into this chamber with another door. I have the key to get past that door and there's this huge room behind it that I use to store all my stuff in. And I'm not saying anymore because it's my secret and Cia's always trying to break into my diary! Jerk!

Anyway, I've been in that room a lot, though, so I might explore the room behind the door in my store room which is behind the chamber in my closet. (Confusing, huh?) Anyway, the room behind my store room is…THE DUNGEON! Scary, huh? Scary works for me and I'm definitely going down there as soon as I can. I'm not scared! (Sort of.)

All right, so that's what I'll do. And I better enjoy the rest of my freedom because it's Sunday and tomorrow is school. 'Go to bed early, you have school!' That's what Mom says and Cia and I say she needs a life. Behind her back, of course. So later!

Be back tomorrow after school,
Karenisha

Saderia stared at the writing, still awestruck that she was able to know what her mother had felt. But mainly she was shocked that her mother had told her what was behind the door in the chamber in her closet. Even more amazing was that there was a *dungeon* somewhere behind that door; the thought sent shivers down Saderia's spine but they were mainly shivers of excitement. And she was also ecstatic that she would have more than just this diary as a link to her mother's past; if she could get past the door in her parents' closet, she would have a whole room of things from her mother's past.

She was amazed that her mother had had school, too, whereas Saderia didn't. She wondered what it was like and if it would be described in there but doubted it. Saderia wished she could go to school and make friends instead of staying locked in her house like a 'good Princess' but pushed her own hopes away and kept reading.

August 21, 1990

Okay, so school wasn't as bad as I led on, but the only reason it wasn't bad or boring like it normally is, is because I made a new friend! Even greater, I made a new friend that Cia doesn't 'approve of' since she's so stuck up. Life doesn't get much better than that!

His name is Makero and he's really nice and smart. He's definitely not as wild as me (like anybody can be!) but we're a good balance. We hung out all day, and I think I finally found someone who doesn't just want to be my friend because I'm going to be Queen one day! Of course, Cia doesn't approve because he's not from this excessively rich family, as is the standard for all her friends. I rolled my eyes at her, and said all her friends were fair-weather friends and I'd be laughing when she figured that out, then otherwise ignored her. The expression she got when I said that was perfect!

Anyway, I forced her to get over it and when we walked home we started daring each other to do things. I won, of course, because Cia's such a chicken. She dared me to climb a tree and roll around in some mud we found and I did it, of course. She was 'disgusted' (her word) but I didn't care and we made it back home. I like doing stuff like that, anything that's fun, but she doesn't. Why, I don't know, but we're as different as day and night. She's been so snobby lately. Maybe it's because Mom told us that because I was older, I was going to get to be Queen. I don't know why she should care, because it's not like I'm looking forward to it. I mean, the entire forest, in my paws, under my control. That's extremely scary.

Anyway, I went in the dungeon yesterday and it was creepy but awesome! I tried to get Cia to go down there but I shouldn't have to tell you that she refused. Wimp. Anyway, I'm not going to say anything about it because it's my secret, still! But I probably won't write here for a while because I've got some serious studying to do, it being one of my last years of high school.

See you _? Studying,
Karenisha

Saderia was surprised to find herself getting to know her mother more within those little paragraphs already and she had thought she would never know things like this about her mom. It was amazing to her, and she greedily kept reading, unaware of the sleep she was missing.

December 1, 1990

Yes, I know, a lot of time has passed and I've been too lazy to write about any of it. Let's just get that fact out of the way and get to the point. The point is that everything's been kind of blah for a while, if you know what I mean. Nothing exciting, just the same old same old stuff. Here's a run-through:

Cia acts all prissy and stereotypical Princess-like and I'm starting to panic because I'm beginning to think I've lost her to the Girly Side. (Shudder.) I've been trying all I can to get Cia to appreciate the better things in life like splashing through water or swinging on trees instead of stupid things like which accessory is best and the latest gossip. I mean, come on! Who in their right mind talks about <u>that</u>? It's sickening!

But I'm sad to report that she's probably too far gone now to be saved, and it is with a heavy heart that I deem my attempts to help her futile.

But depressing stuff aside, I'm having a great time even if I'm constantly bombarded with testing, testing, testing! Ah, the horrors of high school and (shiver) soon college. That's what they're preparing us for, and I use the term 'preparing' loosely. More like 'terrifying!'

Again, scary stuff aside, having a great time because Makero and I always hang out and we're great friends and stuff. We've already made an agreement that we'll survive the remainder of high school together, and help each other study and stuff like this. I consider that brave, but then again, there is (supposedly) a fine line between brave and stupid. Nonetheless, we've studied together and tried to figure out 'what to do with our lives' (Mom and the teacher's words) but we've also found time to hang out together.

AND, on top of the whole studying thing and Cia going over to the dreaded Girly Side, I've also had to deal with a dance this weekend. The dance is TONIGHT! And I've had to deal with it all week. Apparently if you don't go with a date you get to paint an 'L' on your forehead and even though that might not happen to me because I'm still royalty, they all still expect me to go or else I'm a freak of nature, or something like that.

So, I was all prepared to ignore it because dances and stuff like that really aren't my thing, they're Cia's. But, and this was incredibly awkward, Makero asked me to the dance! I swear it was the most awkward and humiliating thing at the time but now I can laugh at it. (Sort of.)   Very last minute, he asked me yesterday, Friday. At first I just stared at him blankly and we just stood there for a while, who knows how long. Then finally, I was able to come up with the incredibly clever response "What?"

He was embarrassed and stuff and so was I when I realized I sounded like a bigger moron than Cia. He reminded me of the dance everyone was talking about and said he was just wondering if I wanted to go with him or not.

Again, I stared at him blankly for a while, but not as long as before. And I was kind of trying to figure out if he was serious or not. When I realized he was, my eyes must have gotten as big as the moon and I said, "You're SERIOUS?! Seriously?!" Then I realized I hurt his feelings and said, "Well, I didn't really mean it like that, just the dance itself. I'm not a dance-ish animal you know." Then I rolled my eyes at myself. I just sounded so stupid.

Anyway, it was incredibly awkward and I'm trying to make up for my 'lack of couth' (Cia's words) and rudeness and started babbling like a moron until I finally just slapped myself in the face and said, "Okay, if you want, you can start running now because I must seem completely crazy, and that's probably not such a bad judgment."

He started laughing and then I did and it was a huge relief to clear the tension. By the way, I am eternally grateful that Cia didn't see this. And when he said he wasn't going to run, I just blurted out, "I'll go..." then started rambling until I finally got myself together.

He said he'd take that as a yes and that he'd come pick me up later on Saturday night and then he left and I ran as fast as I could. And ran right into Cia. And, being as confused as I was then, I exclaimed, "Help me! I'm losing it!"

She said, "Boyfriend troubles?"

I said, "Shut up! He's not my boyfriend and this is not funny!"

She asked me what was going on and I told her everything, finishing with, "And when I talked to him, I sounded just as stupid as you! What is happening to me?!"

She just snorted. "You're in love."

I stared at her blankly, trying to judge whether she was serious and how I should react to this new and incredibly creepy revelation. Eventually, I just started laughing my head off, and laughed all the way home.

Today, I'm not laughing because I actually have to do this and I have no idea what to expect. Cia said she knows what it'll be like but I'm too afraid to ask her. She did tell me that Jash asked her to the dance and we could make it a double date but I told her I'd rather be crushed by a meteor than double date with her and have all my humiliating moments even more publicized than they need to be,. So she just laughed and said we'd split up at the dance. I swear she's mocking me, but I agreed.

It's time to go now and yes, I'm scared, which makes me hyperactive, which isn't going to help the situation.

Well, this should be fun,
Karenisha

Glad that her father was mentioned, too and eager to know what happened, Saderia flipped to the next page and picked up reading.

December 2, 1990

That was so much fun! Shut up, I know how weird that sounds. But the dance really was fun, which I really didn't expect. But, I am also in shock, because of what happened.

Okay, well, what happened was...Makero and I are...dating! Whoa! Cia's getting a good laugh so on top of the shock of having a boyfriend, I have to come up with some way to get her back for laughing at me! Yes, it was another awkward moment that I'm not going to go into this time, and it's weird because I'm excited and alarmed at the same time. Makero really is a cool boyfriend, now, and I finally get to brag to Cia that I'm no longer dateless, so there, but that fact aside, yeah, this is weird.

I feel like I'm being dragged over to the Girly Side and I've made a vow not to go there no matter what's going on with Makero and I. If he doesn't like it, well tough! I'm going to be just as I always was because there is no way I'm going to act like Cia! No way!

The good news is I don't think Makero likes me just because I'm going to control the whole forest when I'm twenty—which is in (yikes!) just four years! And he is sweet and I feel really awkward but can get over that. (I hope.) And so far I've managed not to sound like a complete idiot, just half an idiot. That's progress.

But I'm not having an easy time because I have to worry about, let's see, final grades, upcoming college, Cia, controlling the whole entire forest in just four years when I'm Queen, and now on top of that, a boyfriend. I'm just sixteen!

Life is hard but at least that keeps it interesting.

...

Karenisha

Saderia smiled, about to read more when her eyes flicked to the clock on her bed and she realized what time it was.

"Saderia! Breakfast!" Cia called as she realized it was time for her to wake up.

Reluctantly, Saderia set the diary back into the drawer and got up out of bed to join her aunt and uncle. As she plopped down into her seat at the gold table, the tiredness from staying up from five o'clock in the morning finally got to her and she sagged in her seat with a groan.

Cia looked up at her with concerned blue eyes. "Feeling okay?"

"Just didn't sleep well," Saderia replied.

She gave her a sympathetic look and turned

back to eating.

"Nightmares?" Uncle Jash asked hesitantly.

Saderia shook her head. "Nope. I'm nightmare-free."

"Well, at least that's good," Cia said.

"Yeah," Saderia mumbled.

Inside, Saderia was thinking about her mother's diary and the locked room in her parents' closet. She thought about the door to the other chamber in her parents' closet, and realized that one of the keys she had found in Cia's secret compartment might unlock the door. As she made small talk at the table, she decided she would have to check later that night, since night was the best time for sneaking around the house undetected.

The thought of waiting all day made her very impatient and unhappy, but she decided she would pass the time with reading her mother's diary. She was already hooked into it and was in a hurry to get back to where she had left off.

When she was finally excused from breakfast, it took a lot of discipline not to race to her room and shut the door as tight as it would go. Instead, she walked as casually as possible back to her room where she shut the door quietly, then dove into her bed to pick up reading where she had left off.

A lot of the diary was filled with her mother's achievements and fun times, like when she had gone exploring in the woods for a while, and also how she was having a hard time putting up with Cia. Saderia loved reading about all of it, each word bringing her closer to her mother, until she had to remind herself that she would never see her. When she remembered that fact, coldness spread throughout her body and a lump formed in her throat, making it hard to breathe.

She realized that maybe she shouldn't have read so much about her mother, because every word just made her miss her even more. But she couldn't make herself stop reading it, because she liked the picture it created. She forced herself to accept the pain, actually embracing it so that she could finally fully grieve, she continued reading.

June 27, 1991

Today was my seventeenth birthday and I cannot believe I'm seventeen already! Where did the time go? Mom says I should be really excited because I'm getting closer and closer to being Queen, just three years. I'm not so sure.

Being a Princess never really was my thing and being a Queen is terrifying. I mean, what if I make a mistake? The whole forest will be depending on me, and I just don't know what to do. Cia thinks I'm lucky, and I think she's crazy. I'd gladly hand the title of Queen over to her except that I can't do that and when I tried to, she said no way. She knows it's not as easy as she lets on and I was mad that she acted so calm about it when she wasn't the one who had to do it.

But that's in three years so I'm not too concerned with that whole situation right now. I'm more concerned that when this summer's over I'll be going to college! Scary with a capital S! Mom says I have nothing to worry about but I say I do! By the way, Makero is going with me to college and Cia and Jash are going together. All four of us are going to stick together. Mom and Dad approve of Jash and Makero and I was relieved. Cia acted haughty about it, like 'Of course you approve' but I know she was secretly relieved. We're all sort of a group now and we always hang out. All awkwardness—gone. Thankfully.

Anyway, it was Cia's birthday, too, and I've always hated it that she stole my birthday from me but now I've gotten over it. We don't fight over who gets to have a party anymore, and we just share it. So we both had a private party with Jash and Makero and Mom and Dad and that was it. It was a really cool party and all of us had fun. I liked Cia's present best. It was a trip to the beach for all four of us. Makero, Jash and I all played in the water like kids and none of us felt ashamed.

But Cia mainly stayed out on the beach in the sun which looked sooo boring. We tried to talk her into going into the water but she refused. So we had to get her in the hard way. All three of us went over and dragged Cia in and dunked her under for a minute. She was so mad when we let her up but we convinced her to stay in since she was already wet. We had a great time!

But back to the college thing. More info, please! Mom said I'd have to move out since the closest college is far away from where we live. I about lost it when I heard that and Cia got a little scared, too, but we made a promise to stick together through the whole ordeal. She's a good friend. But anyway, Dad made Cia and I promise to focus on grades. We promised. I meant it, but I don't know about her.

But I really need to get out and enjoy my freedom while it lasts!

College-bound (shiver),
Karenisha

August 21, 1991

I had a great summer. Now I'm terrified.

Today I was supposed to leave for college. Was I scared? OBVIOUSLY! I was petrified! Would you believe that when it was time to leave, I ran to my room and hid in my store room? It happened. I'm serious, too. And make any comment you want about immaturity, but what else was I supposed to do?! I know about a secret room that no one else knows about in my closet, and I'm the only one with keys to it. ... Who in their right mind *wouldn't take it?*

Unfortunately, Mom and Dad and Cia thought ahead and plotted against me. So they told me it was time to leave an hour before it was actually time to leave. So I had to sit in my store room for a whole hour, until I finally decided to give up and come out with my hands up because I was dying of boredom.

They pounced on me before I was even a step out of my room and I'm proud to say I went down fighting! But that didn't really do any good because soon I was on my way to college! They all but chained me to them when we were walking there, but finally I was able to convince them that I wasn't going to try anything crazy such as, but not limited to, run for my life, and I was able to talk to Cia for a while.

"Aren't you afraid?" I asked her.

"No, why should I be?" she asked.

"C-o-l-l-e-g-e," I spelled out, "I'm terrified!"

"Why?"

"Why?! Come on! Why aren't you scared?!"

"Because I know how to act right, how to be popular, how to make friends, and I'm smart."

"Oh, yeah, and you're implying I'm not?!"

"Yes," she said, stifling a laugh.

I glared at her but soon we met up with Makero and Jash and that's where Mom and Dad left us, trusting us to continue to college. Well, actually they probably trusted Cia, Makero and Jash to drag me there, but I let myself think that wasn't the case.

They didn't have to drag me; I went willingly. We talked and they were a little scared, as I finally got them to admit. But soon we were at college and discovered it wasn't so bad.

I'm there now, studying with Makero while Cia and Jash are out talking to animals or something. Probably won't write here for a while.

I survived!
Karenisha

Saderia was called to the dining room to eat lunch, which she gulped down quickly, so as to return to her room as fast as possible. Once she was back in her room, she immediately started reading again, desperate to see how her mother's story ended, and not wanting to think about how it *really* ended.

May 30, 1995

I've graduated from college with a 4.0 average (which was hard). Makero got the same average as me and Cia and Jash got 3.5 averages (ha ha). College was actually pretty fun, but now that I've graduated, I'm actually looking forward to being Queen. I've always wanted to help, I guess, and even though it is scary, it'll be great to be able to help my forest. This is so great!

More news! Two days before the graduation ceremony, Makero proposed to me and now we're engaged to be married soon. This is incredible and I almost can't believe it! And Jash proposed to Cia a while before, so they're going to be married, too. This time SHE told ME that she was scared and I said I'd be there for her... to laugh at her mistakes. Hey, it's only fair. But I confessed I was scared too and she promised to be there to laugh, too. We hugged and cried like excited twin sisters, but I made sure no one saw first, even though it was nice.

I'm twenty years old now. I'm Queen and I rule the forest now. It's amazing, but right now I'm just happy about going home! Mom and Dad will be so happy to see me!

Homecoming,
Karenisha

As Saderia turned to the next page, she immediately caught a few of the words and her mouth gaped in an O shape. She immediately began to read the page, anxious to know if this was what she thought it was, and if it had anything to do with the little things she had found out on the internet about it. Her heart began to beat faster as she read.

June 3, 1995

I'm Queen of the forest now and going to be married soon. And as if that isn't exciting enough, Mom has to tell me some new, huge royal family secret. At first I couldn't believe it but then I realized that it must be true.

First of all, sorry, but I can't say a lot about it because it is very, very, VERY secret. I'm not allowed to tell anyone outside the royal family and it's advised that I don't tell anyone within it, either. Since I'm part of the royal family and Queen, it's best that I keep it to myself since I'm the only one who really needs it. Mom didn't tell Dad, and I'm advised not to tell Makero, or even Cia!

The huge secret has to do with the tomb of my oldest ancestor, Queen Tarae, the one who started the entire royal family line. I know a bit about her, but I don't even know if I should talk about that. But basically, the secret is that Queen Tarae had this…power (I can't say what), and she used that power to rule the forest really well. She wanted to let her children have that power to make wise decisions to help the forest, but she didn't know if it was a trait that would pass on, so she left something in the tomb to give her children the power.

Well, the first few generations of my ancestors had to use this thing to get the power but after a while, it did pass on through the royal family as a trait. So it was kind of forgotten except for the Queen or King of the royal family passing it on to the Prince or Princess. It can never get into the wrong hands because really bad things could happen, I don't know exactly what but it would be awful, so it's best to keep the information in our heads, and tell no one.

Oh, and Mom also said that I'm the 49ᵗʰ generation, whatever that means. She told me that there was something important about the next generation but she didn't know exactly why; none of the royal family before her knew exactly why either. All she could tell me was that there was something special about the daughter of the 50th generation. I guess I missed being that, but does that mean that if I have a daughter she'll be special?

Anyway, the tomb is locked and I was told how to open it and that is the secret that I can tell no one. Mom said I could tell Cia or Makero about the first part if I really wanted to, but not even them about this next part. I can't write it down because of the secrecy and I understand why it could be dangerous in the wrong hands.

I sort of have the power but it's not as good as it could be. Maybe my future daughter will have better luck. But anyway, I can't write down any more information and I have to keep it in my head forever. Mom instructed me to pass this information down to my child when I have one, which I'm supposed to do and which I want to do, and tell her never to tell anyone, like I was told. I sure wish I had more info about this 'daughter of the 50th generation' thing. Will my future child really be special?

Secretive,
Karenisha

Saderia stared at the page for a long time, letting the words sink in. So her mother had known the code to the lock on the tomb, but had told no one, not even Cia, so, like her, it was quickly and unexpectedly lost forever. She let out a sad sigh but quickly picked up on something else that caught her attention.

She was the 'daughter of the 50th generation' her mother had mentioned? It said in the diary that that meant she was supposed to be somehow special and for a moment she felt a glimmer of hope, but then it faded. She knew of no way that she was special or different from anybody else. She didn't even think she had the power mentioned in the diary, and she could never get it because the tomb would forever be locked. She was just an ordinary tiger, albeit a Princess, but unlike the royal tigers before her because she didn't have the secret power and never would.

She was called to dinner which was frustrating because she was desperate to keep reading and know more, but she got through it and returned to her room.

Turning her attention back to the book she read the last few entries.

June 20, 1995

I went to Cia and Jash's wedding and my sister looked so happy! It was very heartwarming and even our teasing was heartfelt! It was sort of a private wedding with just me, Makero, Mom and Dad, and the bride and groom of course. Whoa, I have a brother-in-law!

It was the stuff dreams are made of, Cia told me. I agreed completely, loving how happy my sister was and how close we and our little group of four are. She was ecstatic and now I'm even more excited and anxious for my wedding!

It was a lot of fun! It was a beautiful moment (and no one saw me tearing up, I don't think!) and I ate lots of cake afterward. We all made a toast and gave them presents.

I was a little scared that Cia would be mad that I got to be Queen but she wasn't and she said it was all right...as long as she got to stay in the house. I laughed and agreed quickly, because I couldn't imagine living in a house without my sister. Everything was perfect.

For Cia and Jash,

Saderia realized that she shared in her mother's and Cia's happiness, as expressed on the page and turned to the next page, smiling when she saw that it was the day of her mother and father's wedding.

June 30, 1995

Today was the day of my wedding. I was so nervous but Cia told me that it would be okay and so I relaxed and immediately felt happy. Just Cia, Jash and Mom and Dad were there to see our wedding. I liked the privacy and I think Makero did, too.

It went perfectly and that's all I can say. Cia cried, denying it later, and Mom cried, too, and we got showered in presents and it was amazing. The wedding cake tasted wonderful and Cia made a toast to us. It was great. My dreams our coming true!

For us,
Karenisha

The next few pages were brief descriptions of what it was like to be Queen and how her mother had to deal with advisors and stuff since she was a new Queen. As she turned to the next page, something caught her eye, and she read it closely, starting to feel colder with unease.

May 7, 1996

Today was a strange day, and I know I probably messed up really bad. I never have been able to say the right things but it was such a shock! Anyway, this is what happened.

Dastarius, one of my most trusted advisors, has been helping us adjust a little. There's so much stuff to cover and so many problems to take care of. We've been doing pretty well so far and I'm glad to be able to help my forest, but it's a little overwhelming. Anyway, Dastarius must have guessed how overwhelmed we were, and said something totally unexpected.

We were all at the meeting place and he suggested that he could take over part of the forest! He explained that he would be doing us a favor until we knew what we were doing more, but I was shocked! Makero was a little angry since it sort of sounded like he didn't think we were a competent King and Queen but mainly we were just surprised. I reacted too quickly and told him there was no way that would happen, but I know I said the wrong things and ended up humiliating him.

He left the meeting after that. I tried to apologize and make up for what was said even though I knew it would be useless, but it didn't exactly come out right. Dastarius said it was fine, though, and that he'd still be an advisor. Still, I don't think we'll see him around for a while. (Sigh). I hope this Queen stuff gets easier.

New Queen,
Karenisha

Saderia immediately felt her suspicions and anger rise at Dastarius for what he had done, as she stared at the page. Instantly, her thoughts began to swirl around her suspicion as she thought about it. Control of the forest could go *only* to the royal family and *no one* else. It was her parents' forest to rule, and he had no right to take it from them! Was *that* what he was trying to do?!

She hissed, thinking that she had been right all along about Dastarius, though she didn't know what she had been right about, just that there was something wrong about him. Then she realized she was overreacting, just like her mother had. The way it was written made it sound like he was actually trying to help and her mother had made a mistake. With a sigh, she dropped her suspicions, knowing that she had reacted too quickly and made assumptions, just like her mother had. What he'd done was probably harmless, but she didn't like to admit it.

Pushing it out of her mind, Saderia turned her attention to the next page, the last page in the diary, then blinked in surprise when she caught sight of the date. It was her birthday.

June 11, 1996

This is probably the happiest moment of my life! I have a little baby girl named Saderia and I have never known a joy as pure as this! She is gorgeous and has a beautiful fluffy tail--just like her Mom! I'm a Mom now! I wish only the best for her and I hope her life is filled with adventure, friends, happiness, and truth.

I know she will be smart and adventurous, kind but bold, and a truth-seeker. I don't know how, but I can just tell already. Makero was so excited, too, and he loves baby Saderia. He told me he always wanted a daughter, just like me, and I couldn't have been happier! Cia and Jash are so happy for us and they love little Saderia, too.

This is a wonderful time! And I've already decided that when she gets older, I'm going to give her this diary to finish it, and record the events of her life in it. Cia, Jash and Makero and I love her very much, and there are almost no words for it!

For Baby Saderia,
Karenisha

Saderia blinked away tears as she read the passage over and over. Her mother loved her. Her father loved her. Even Cia and Uncle Jash did, it said. And suddenly she knew she had to know more about the horrible fire that took them away. She didn't know why and it was definitely a troubling and upsetting thought, whenever her mind drifted to that horrible day, but something inside her was driving her to find out. Without thinking, she flipped to the front page of the diary and read, "Trust your intuition," one of the rules her mother had written and valued.

Without a doubt, she knew that she had to find out more, but she couldn't do it now. She was going to stick to her plans to go into her mother's store room and maybe even the dungeon tonight, using Cia's keys, but tomorrow after she had completed the lessons her tutors gave her and completed her homework, she would find some way to know more about that grim day.

Chapter Six

The Lying Library

Saderia jumped when she heard Cia's voice call, "Saderia! Time for bed!"

"Okay, Cia!" she called back, scrambling to hide her mother's diary back in the drawer and flick the lights out at the same time. When she slammed the drawer shut, she quickly pulled the blanket over her and pretended to be on the verge of sleep.

Cia and Uncle Jash came in a moment later. Her uncle hovered in the doorway while Cia came over to say goodnight. When she pretended to be falling asleep, they left and Saderia stayed put for another long, boring hour until she was sure they were asleep and wouldn't catch her sneaking around.

Without another thought, Saderia got out of bed and fumbled around in the drawer for the ring of keys she had found in Cia's room. She rushed hastily out of her room, down the hall and then over to her parents' room on the other hall, opening the door without hesitation. She slid into the closet naturally and flicked on the light with her tail to help her see the hidden door in the back. Once inside the little chamber, she went to the huge, locked door and began trying different keys to open it.

The second one she tried worked and anticipation tickled her mind as she shoved against the door as hard as she could to force it open. Even unlocked, that was a difficult task but eventually she pushed it aside enough for her to get through. But the door let out a loud groan. Saderia froze, listening intently for any sounds indicating that Cia and Uncle Jash had woken up, but there was nothing.

Breathing a sigh of relief when she was sure she was safe, she slipped through the huge door and her mouth fell open as she took in the scene in front of her. There were stacks of old toys, presents, sports stuff and many other keepsakes. There were shelves and shelves of papers: letters, notes, schoolwork, and much more!

She walked around the dimly lit room, looking through her mother's old things. There were piles of adventure books and mystery novels along with a few old movies, though it was clear that her mother had favored the written word. She sifted through the stacks of paper and saw stories probably written for an English class and complicated problems from a math class, along with many other things that reflected her mother's schooling. There were pictures of her mother in the forest, at parties, with Cia, with Makero and countless other photos.

Saderia was fascinated as she took in the hundreds of keepsakes from her mother's old life, wondering how she could ever go through it all, but then her eyes stopped on a smooth, but faded wooden case on one wall of the room. She started toward it and looked through the glass door to see four pictures. They all had a film of dust on them, but one looked newer than the others.

The picture on the left was of her mother and Cia in the forest. The one on the right was of her mother and father. The middle one on the left was of her mother and father and Cia and Uncle Jash at the beach. The middle one on the right, the newer one, was a picture of a baby tiger, and she knew that it was herself.

But she was mainly focused on the single sheet of paper propped up in the case. It read:

My Dreams

These are the dreams that I, Karenisha, have for my future.

1. I want to have a fun life and take risks, not just living in a boring world.

2. I want to explore as many places as possible and learn as much as I can about my forest and the world.

3. I want to get good grades in school, from kindergarten to college.

4. I want to be a good Princess, but one who helps animals and solves problems, not one who takes orders and 'knows her place.' Later, I want to be a good Queen with enough common sense and knowledge to be able to help others and make my forest as good and safe as possible.

5. I want to make friends.

6. I want to always be friends with Cia and I want her to help me out when I become Queen. I want us to stick together always.

7. I want to find out about my ancestors and the history of my royal family.

8. I want to have an adventurous life with friends by my side.

9. I want to probably get married someday, although the details for that are a little sketchy now.
10. I want to have a daughter someday. I know for certain that this is definitely what I want. I want her life to be wonderful, and I want her to fulfill as many of these dreams, as well as her own, even if I don't. I want to be able to help her and teach her and do whatever I can to make her life great. I want her name to be Saderia.

Her eyes widened as she read the last dream and she felt her heart skip a beat. A warm, but sorrow-tinged feeling spread over her as she realized just how much her mother must have cared about her. Briefly, she envisioned the life she would have had, had her parents been in it, but it hurt too much to know that that would never be. She smiled weakly, but had to move away from the glass case.

Pulling herself together, she saw an even heavier door at the back of the room and realized that that must be the door to the dungeon. Suddenly she felt afraid of going down there and wished she had brought a flashlight, but started toward it nonetheless, swallowing her fear. The key that had opened the first door opened that one, and Saderia had to use all of her might to push it open.

Eventually it fell open to a dark, dusty staircase leading down into the dungeon. The stairs spiraled away from her, behind a wall, so that she couldn't see where she would end up. A trickle of fear shivered down her spine but she kept going. As she spiraled downward with the stairs, she had to squint to make out the way in front of her through the unending darkness. The stairs were hard, dusty, and creaked every time she put weight on them, but they didn't have that dank, disgusting feel to them that she would have assumed a dungeon would have.

When she finally reached the bottom, she could make out thick, iron bars marking different cells down a long narrow way in the dungeon. All of them were empty, having gone unused for many centuries but they had the lingering trace of fear. The rest of the dungeon was like the stairs, frightening but not horrifying. There were chains in the cells, but that seemed typical of a thousand-years-old dungeon. Saderia was afraid, but not petrified, and found that she was able to move down the line of cells, looking into each one as she made her way to a door at the end, growing increasingly curious as to what was inside. As she walked she noticed unlit torches lining the walls but suddenly she was standing in front of the door at the end of the dungeon.

This door was unlocked and when she shoved hard enough, she got it to open without a sound. When she peeked inside, it felt a lot safer than the dungeon behind her, but there was only a pedestal in the middle of the tiny room with a large scroll sitting neatly on top of it. A feather pen laid beside it, still with ink in it to write with. An unlit candle was also nearby, but unusable after so much time had passed. Saderia didn't need it, though, as her amber eyes slowly adjusted to the darkness around her, and she gently nudged the scroll with her nose, making it elegantly unroll at her touch.

Her eyes grew wider as she took in the contents of the scroll, which was so long it rolled down to her feet. She looked closely at the lines scratched across the scroll and was surprised at how they remained so clear after so much time. On the scroll was written:

The Royal Family Tree

Queen Tarae-King Macedoniay

|

Queen Taharah-King Hyeran

|

King Malinkta-Queen Lesique

|

King Lerik-Queen Hemeria

The scroll continued on for several generations in the carefully placed, neat handwriting. Saderia was very aware of Queen Tarae's name at the top and remembered all that she had learned about her and her tomb. She skimmed the rest of the long scroll, looking over the many names of Kings and Queens of long, long ago.

She figured out the two lines connecting two

names meant that they were married and then the one vertical line meant that the next names were their children. For sisters and brothers, there was one line connecting them, and two diagonal lines from the parents.

Continuing to follow the ancient lines and script of ancient animals, she finally came to the bottom of the scroll where the names stopped. Forty-nine generations of her family stood on the paper, and so the last names on the scroll were exactly what she would have expected.

Queen Milieton-King Kaleron
/ \
Jash-Cia-- Queen Karenisha-King Makero

Saderia stared at her mother and father's names along with her aunt and uncle's and sighed, wishing they could all be together, all five of them. Without even realizing what she was doing, Saderia took the feather pen and wrote her own name underneath Karenisha and Makero's names, being careful to copy the neat handwriting to the best of her ability and drawing a vertical line to her name when she was finished.

She studied her name for a moment:

Princess Saderia

While the ink was drying, she quickly smudged out the Princess part. She was about to write Queen, since she would be a Queen one day and the scroll seemed to record it that way, but then dropped the pen and waited for the ink to dry on just her name. She was a Princess, but she wasn't defined by it. She was Saderia, and that was all she ever wanted to be.

Her eyes skipped over the generations one last time, hers being the fiftieth generation of the royal family, then rolled up the scroll to put it back where she had found it. She stepped out of the room, soundlessly closing the door behind her as she raced back up the stairs and pulled the huge metal door shut with great effort. Casting one last glance around at the store room, she left that behind too, locking the chamber door behind her then leaving the closet, the room, and retreating once more.

After putting the keys away, she curled up in her bed under the blanket and started crying silently. She didn't know why but it felt good to just get it out of her system. After a few moments she realized why she was crying and let out a long, teary sigh. Her mother had wanted Saderia to fulfill as many of the dreams she had listed as possible, had hoped and counted on her to succeed at them, but in ten years of life she hadn't done a single one.

The next morning, she awoke to Cia's usual breakfast call and then sat through an extremely boring lecture from her tutors, nodding at the appropriate times and giving the correct answer, barely having to think at all except about how to survive it. She was even more impatient than usual because she desperately wanted to get to the library to look up information about the fire. She didn't want to use the computer at her house for fear that Cia or Uncle Jash would catch her.

She sped through her homework as fast as possible, jotting down any answer that came to mind and probably getting most of them wrong. She hissed in frustration when Cia and Uncle Jash called her to lunch but put on a smile as she walked into the room and took her seat.

"So how are you doing with your tutors?" Cia asked. "You're paying more attention, right?"

She nodded, itching to run from the room. "Yes, Cia. I'm doing well. I understand more now," she hedged.

"That's good," Uncle Jash spoke up. "Do you need help with anything, though?"

"I work better on my own," Saderia told them.

"Oh…okay."

Too late she realized that what she said had come out too harshly but she couldn't take it back now and she was in a hurry to finish and get to the library.

"Are you in a hurry for something?" Cia asked curiously.

"I, uh, I want to go to the library," Saderia said quickly, making up an excuse as she went. "I'm in a hurry because...I just realized the book I have is overdue and I want to return it quickly."

"You won't get in any trouble. You're a Princess."

"Yeah, I know but...I don't...want to make a bad image for myself by making it seem like I'm above the rules for the others. I'm trying to be like a role model," Saderia came up with as fast as she could.

"That's a good idea," Uncle Jash said. "That's smart."

Saderia tried to smile back at him then turned to Cia as she said, "Yes, it is a good idea. But a few minutes more to finish your lunch won't hurt."

"I know," Saderia agreed, keeping the reluctance out of her voice.

As she hurried to finish her food without making it seem like she was hurrying, she made conversation with her aunt and uncle, trying to seem light and normal. She was grateful when she was finished with her food and was excused from the table.

"Wait," Cia said. "Are you going to bring some books back?"

"Um, yeah," Saderia said. "Reading helps me learn."

"Okay, wait there a minute. I'll get you a bag to help you carry them in."

Saderia waited as patiently as possible as Cia walked out of the dining room and came back a moment later carrying a faded blue bag in her teeth. "Here you go," she said, handing it to Saderia.

Uncle Jash looked at the bag in surprise as it was presented to her. "That was Karenisha's," he blurted out.

Saderia turned to look at him in surprise, instinctively gripping the bag tighter in her teeth.

Cia shot him a hard look. "I just grabbed whatever I saw. Yes, it was Karenisha's, but what does it matter?"

Everything, Saderia thought. "Can I keep it?" she blurted out.

"Um...sure, I guess," Cia said.

"Thanks, Cia. Bye, guys." She nosed her head under the strap, draping it around her neck as she padded off toward her room to get a book to return and use as her excuse, smiling down at the blue bag. When she reached her room, she quickly opened the drawer where she kept the book she had been reading, and began digging through its contents.

A few things fell out of the drawer and Saderia quickly picked up a pencil and her mother's diary and put them back, seeing nothing else although she swore that something else had fallen. Forgetting it, she grabbed the book when it was finally discovered and dropped it in the bag. She closed the drawer tightly then walked out of the room and out of the house, calling a last goodbye to her aunt and uncle.

As soon as she was out of eyesight, she started running down the dirt path to another part of the forest where the library and a few other public places were located. She slowed down as she walked through the doors of the library and was welcomed by many shelves of books with a calm atmosphere. A few animals were checking out books or reading at tables and Saderia waved to them when they bowed or curtsied, ignoring her annoyance at how differently she was treated because of her title. She quickly returned the book she had brought and then went deeper into the comforting shelves.

She made her way over to the row of computers lining one wall, all of them free of other animals to her relief. She sat on the far end, not wanting to be disturbed, and falteringly began typing in the words '1996 Fire' and adding her parents name after a pause. Search results flooded the page and she clicked on the first one she saw, having to start somewhere. Tuning out the rest of the world, she began to read.

1996 Fire
Kills Queen Karenisha and King Makero

On November 17, 1996, a huge fire was

started near the King and Queen's den, spreading extremely quickly to other places and gaining incredible heights up the trees. The smoke was thick and it covered the entire west part of the forest, where the King and Queen lived secluded, away from the town.

The fire came dangerously close to the King and Queen's den, and a wall of fire separated the house from other parts of the forest. The way the fire started was too quick and too explosive, and the way it spread, as if in specific patterns, was suspicious.

Saderia stared at the screen with a growing sense of horror. What was being implied here? She was almost afraid to know, but continued reading.

Queen Karenisha and King Makero tried to put out the fire but in doing so, got trapped on the other side of the wall of flame where no one could help them. They were killed in the fire, their bodies thought to have been too badly burned to be recovered. It took many hours to put out the fire and many animals were injured in trying.

Queen Cia and King Jash took Karenisha and Makero's place as the new rulers of the forest when it was clear they were dead.

After the fire, there was a weak smell of gasoline in the air, and it made sense because of how quickly and without warning the

```
fire started and spread. No traces of a match
or something to ignite the flame were found
but it could have easily been burned away.
    It is a theory that somebody might have
started the fire to kill the King and Queen.
However, no evidence or suspects were ever
found.
```

Saderia's eyes widened and a sick feeling churned her stomach. Horror washed over her as she realized that what was said made sense. Somebody could have killed her parents! Then, just as suddenly as horror and sadness had come over her, a rage unlike any she had ever felt before blocked out every thought she had so that only one remained: she *had* to find out who did this, and make them pay.

Then she realized how hopeless that was when nothing had been found out about it in ten years. She let out a sigh, but couldn't ease the burning anger that made her have to grit her teeth to keep herself in control. If somebody really had killed her parents and taken away the life she could have had with them, they would pay.

Trying not to break the keys, she clicked out of that link to see if any of the others said the same as it. When she looked at the next link, though, her fists went slack and her body went numb with horror at what was written.

1996 Fire Kills Horrible King and Queen

1996 was the day a forest fire started in the west side of the forest, where the King and Queen lived separate from the rest of the forest. The fire was easily put out and only a few animals were hurt by it. It was clearly started by natural causes or a careless mistake.

The fire killed two animals: King Makero and Queen Karenisha, two of the worst rulers in history. King Makero and Queen Karenisha never did anything for their forest; all they ever cared about were themselves. While others suffered, they did nothing about it and let many animals die, when it was their job to protect them. Their reign was short, though, because of the fire.

Saderia could do nothing but stare as the words sunk into her, fueling her rage. Why had this website gone out of its way to insult her parents? It was so unlike the other one she had read, and it basically claimed the fire was no big deal. It *was*, and she knew just how big a deal it was. She remembered it only too well and it was the worst thing she had ever seen, much worse than any fire before it, she guessed.

She wondered why the two websites would differ so much, almost as if this one were trying to draw attention away from the fire and make it seem unimportant. But why?

Clicking on the next link, she read:

1996 Fire
The Fire: A forest fire started in the west
part of the forest and was put out quickly
and easily. It only killed two animals and
was just a natural problem in the forest that
was quickly and easily dealt with.
Animals Killed: King Makero and Queen Karenisha were killed in the fire, but no one else.
Two Horrible Rulers: Karenisha and Makero
were horrible rulers who did nothing for
their forest. An example of this would be
another fire in 1995, when they did nothing
to help while animals died. Thankfully, others stepped in to help, but the King and
Queen hardly noticed. They were lazy, unintelligent and self-centered.

Saderia was aghast that both websites had said such horrible things and made the fire sound so simple, and not the horrifying, terrifying disaster it really was. She clicked through several other links, scanning them quickly with her eyes but they all said the same awful things as the last two.

She couldn't help a trickle of doubt from entering her mind and shaking her faith that the websites were lies. When there were so many of them, one after another of horrible things about her parents, how could it possibly *not* be true? Were her parents not what she remembered; had she just wanted to remember them that way even when she had somehow known the truth? She had thought she knew them so well but maybe...

Then she remembered all of the things she had found out about her parents. Her mother's list of dreams and the way she described things in her diary. The pictures of her mother and Cia and Uncle Jash and her father, all together and happy. Her mother had written that she wanted to help animals as best as she could and Saderia couldn't picture the animal who had wrote the diary as being the same one that was described in the websites.

Just because they were good animals didn't mean they were good rulers, a voice in her mind said. But she refused to listen to it, recalling everything she remembered and everything she had learned. Some mistakes had probably been made, but then animals always made mistakes. The purpose of them was to learn from them and she was certain her mother and father had been great leaders of the forest.

But then why had the websites said such horrible, untrue things? She wanted to believe that the animals who created them just hadn't been able to see the real leaders that they were, because of their short leadership, but she couldn't help but think that there was something else. She thought about how it toned down the awful disaster that claimed her parents' lives so that it seemed like a simple kitchen fire. What was going on?

She clicked up the link that had implied that the

fire had been planned and studied it for a long time. So intent on the computer type, she didn't notice when someone had come up behind her until a voice made her jump.

"Find something interesting, Princess?"

"Dastarius!" she squeaked as she jumped and whirled around in her chair, nearly falling out of it.

Dastarius raised an eyebrow. "Sorry, I didn't mean to startle you."

"It-it's...okay," Saderia said, trying to slow down her heart rate. "What are you doing here?"

"Just looking something up," he replied coolly.

Saderia stopped herself from asking what, uncomfortably aware of how weird she was acting.

"What are you doing here?" Dastarius asked her. "Research for something?"

Without giving her a chance to protest he looked at the website she was on, rolling her chair out of the way carefully with his paw.

"You can't do that!" Saderia protested, although too late because he had already finished reading the information on the screen.

Dastarius looked at her calmly, with an amused expression. "You act like I pushed you out of a window, rather than pushed your chair out of the way."

Infuriated, Saderia jumped off the chair and clicked out of the website, even though it was too late to hide it. "What I look at is *my* business," she hissed. "You have no right to come over here and spy."

"Spy?" His gaze softened, but just slightly. He let it drop and said instead, "You wanted to know about the fire that took your parents."

"Maybe," Saderia growled, looking away from him.

"It wasn't a question."

After a long, silent moment Saderia finally turned back around to face him with narrowed eyes. "So what?" she hissed. "I think I deserve to know what happened."

"I never said you didn't," he replied coolly. He glanced back at the blank computer screen and suddenly his voice was serious. "The one website you were on implied that someone purposely started the fire."

"Really? I hadn't noticed," Saderia snapped sarcastically. She glared at him, but then pleaded more desperately, "That couldn't really happen, could it? I mean, who would kill them?"

Dastarius was silent for a moment, as if debating what to tell her. "They were the King and Queen," he said finally. "The King and Queen have a lot of power and control but with that comes danger. I think they were well aware of the danger when they took their titles."

"But *why* would anyone do that?!" Saderia exclaimed.

"Who knows?" Dastarius said with a sigh. "Maybe some animal was angry with the way they were ruling the forest. Maybe an action they did that was meant to help ended up hurting someone else. Or," he said, seeming to be deep in thought, "they could have been killed by an animal seeking power. King and Queen are powerful roles, and a lot of animals would do anything to get it. Maybe they thought that if the King and Queen were gone, they could take their place."

"But that's stupid!" Saderia protested. "Only animals in the royal family can become King or Queen!"

Dastarius nodded. "You're right. I suppose..." Suddenly he stopped and his face seemed to get darker.

"What?" Saderia asked suspiciously, although she wasn't sure if she wanted to know what he was thinking.

"Only the royal family can become King and Queen," Dastarius repeated, his tone still calm but his face dark and serious. "Your mother, Queen Karenisha, was older so she was the one who was supposed to become Queen. But if something were to happen to her before you, the royal heir, grew old enough to take her place, her sister, Cia, would take her place and become Queen."

Saderia felt cold claws reaching toward her heart. "What are you implying?" she asked, her voice trembling slightly.

Dastarius looked her in the eye, but it was as if he were looking through her to something else entirely. Transfixed, Saderia stared back into his glinting amber eyes. "Cia might not have gotten much say in what happened since she wasn't Queen," Dastarius began. "She could have been jealous that the title was taken from her so easily, just because she had an older sister. Or maybe Jash didn't like that he and Cia didn't get as much control as Karenisha and Makero. They knew that they would be King and Queen if Karenisha and Makero were gone…"

"They didn't do anything!" Saderia protested, angry now. "You can't accuse them of that! Karenisha was Cia's sister, and that's stronger than some stupid ambition! You don't know anything! They didn't kill them!" She whispered the last part, glaring at him hatefully. "What right do you have to come into my life and accuse them of that?!"

"Calm down," Dastarius told her. "I'm not accusing them or anybody of anything. I'm just thinking."

"Well, you're wrong! Cia's not…!"

"I never said that Cia or Jash did it. I'm just pointing out a possibility. Don't get too upset about it." He paused then added, "But just think about it for a while. It makes the most sense."

"I don't have to listen to you!" Saderia hissed. But inside, she was horrified because it *did* make sense! Cia and Uncle Jash *had* become King and Queen after the fire and the way one site said that it was planned made her instantly suspicious. Could it be true…? Was she living with murderers?!

"You don't have to listen, Princess, but it might

help if you did," Dastarius told her coolly.

"It wouldn't help at all!" Saderia shouted.

Suddenly the librarian, a panther, came around to tell them to be quiet but stopped when she saw who it was.

"Oh, Princess Saderia," she murmured, "Dastarius." She seemed embarrassed and uncomfortable, but openly curious.

"We'll speak quieter," Dastarius said smoothly with a glance at Saderia. "We're just discussing royal business." He looked at the panther in a way that told her she was supposed to leave.

"Oh, okay…" the librarian trailed off as she moved away from them quickly.

"Stop manipulating everyone," Saderia hissed at him, looking at him with narrowed eyes.

"What do you mean 'manipulating?'" Dastarius asked, sounding surprised.

Saderia shook her head. "Never mind." Because she really didn't know why she had said it because it didn't *seem* like he was doing that. She had always guessed that something like manipulation would be a bit more obvious, but she just had this feeling. But she had no proof and could put no words to it. Besides, she was glad that the attention drawn to them was gone, though she felt a little uneasy with no one around.

"Anyway, I'm just trying to figure out what could have happened," Dastarius picked up where their conversation had left off. "I'm not accusing anybody."

"Fine," Saderia muttered, "but that's not what happened."

Dastarius didn't look about to argue and instead said, "I need to go. I hope you find what you were looking for."

"Thanks," Saderia replied tartly, waiting for him to leave.

Dastarius smiled in a way that seemed like a smirk then turned to leave. "Oh, and Princess?" he called over his shoulder.

Saderia looked up at him with narrowed eyes. "Don't call me that," she snapped.

Dastarius ignored that and went on. "If you ever feel like you're in danger, I'm only here to help." Then he walked away from her as she stared after him, fear making her blood run cold.

The way he had said it so seriously gave her shivers, as if he really believed that something might happen to her. She didn't have to wonder about that much because she could easily guess that he meant Cia and Uncle Jash and what he had said about them...killing her parents. Dark thoughts swirled around in her mind. Could they have really killed her mother and father just to become King and Queen? The Cia and Uncle Jash she knew were annoying sometimes, but she had never thought they could be killers.

Trying desperately to erase those dark thoughts from her mind, she turned back to the computer, wishing she hadn't clicked off of it so quickly. But she had definitely read enough from there, and she returned to her previous problem of how badly the websites spoke of her parents. A part of her knew it couldn't be true and there was something bad going on, but another part of her was scared that it might be right. She didn't want to explore for fear of knowing that what was said online was correct, but her curiosity drove her to think it through.

She would focus on the things about her parents first, and she immediately knew of one way to check the truth. Her parents, having been the King and Queen, were important and respected, so there must be a few biographies on them, and she *was* in a library.

"Miss," she called, walking toward the panther librarian who was stacking books on one of the shelves.

The panther looked up at her, curiosity from what she had witnessed earlier still clear in her eyes. But she curtsied formally when she saw the Princess. "Princess Saderia," she said, "what can I do for you?"

"Can you tell me where to find biographies?" Saderia asked politely.

The librarian pointed it out to her then said, "Do you need any help finding something?"

"No, that's all right. Thank you." Saderia smiled sweetly at her and then walked off toward a shelf up against one wall. She quickly began scanning the books for her parents' names, but frowned when she couldn't find any. She checked the books again, pulling out some that looked promising but then putting them back, discouraged. After the fourth check, she knew there were none there, and hissed in fury.

She had thought for sure that there would be some books on the previous King and Queen, and there were books about some of the other Kings and Queens of the past, but none of her parents. Weren't they worth mentioning? If they were so terrible, wouldn't that be worth recording? The fire at least should have gained them some fame even if the thought infuriated Saderia.

Briefly she thought of asking the librarian about it but decided against it. The librarian would probably just pity her for wanting to know about her parents, offering no information, and Saderia didn't want anyone's pity.

Still frustrated, Saderia began pulling the books off the shelf, sitting back on three paws, hoping that there would be something about her parents hidden behind them. Maybe a book got pushed to the back and she just couldn't see it. As soon as she cleared the top shelf she put them all back, finding nothing. Then she moved on to the next shelf and reassembled the books in the right order when she found nothing.

But then she started on the right side of the next shelf. Pulling away several books, she saw something on the other side that was not a book, but a lot more curious. Peering more closely at what she had uncovered she was shocked to see that it was a handle with a lock on it. Instantly, Saderia was transported back to the time when she had discovered the secret compartment in Cia's closet and the secret door in her mother's closet. She wondered if she had found another secret room in the library, but then realized how far-fetched that was because she could see the door more clearly, now that the books were gone, and apart from the shelf, nothing was hiding it.

But why *was* the shelf in front of it? She knew it shouldn't strike her as so strange but a feeling told her that there was more to what she was seeing than she thought. Recalling what her mother had wrote, *trust your intuition*, she decided she had to get inside to check it out. But when she turned the handle it was locked tight and she sighed, wondering why everything in her life was nothing but a locked door.

Her feeling screamed at her to find some way to open it but there was no way, because she didn't have the key, and how else was she supposed to get in there? Why should she even care? She turned away to put the books back and go home when a glitter from inside the blue bag she had borrowed caught her eye. Frowning in confusion, she opened the bag and peeked inside. Then she gaped in shock when she saw what had grabbed her attention: Cia's ring of keys.

She carefully picked them up and turned them

around in bewilderment, trying to figure out how they had gotten there and feeling a little spooked. Then she recalled when she had dug for the book in her drawer and something fell. The keys must have fallen out with the other things and landed in her bag, she realized. But then her eyes drifted back to the handle of the hidden door. She looked back at the keys and wonder came over her.

"Could it be…?" she murmured. There was no way what she was thinking could be true. But she had to try anyway, and after glancing around swiftly, seeing no one, she turned back to the door to stick the first key in the lock.

She sucked in a quick breath when she heard the lock click and when she turned the handle, she was able to push it back a little. It had opened. Dropping the keys back in the bag, she looked around again to make sure no one was looking then slowly and carefully began to push her side against the bookshelf and move it just enough out of the way that she could slip behind it. It made no sound, much to Saderia's relief, and she silently pushed the door open then pulled it shut softly.

Saderia closed her eyes for a moment, listening for any noise suggesting someone had seen her, and then when she was sure she was free of suspicion, she wondered how *Cia*'s keys could have possibly opened up a locked door in the *library*. Where had she gotten the keys and why did she have them? It sort of made sense that they might have something like that, being King and Queen, but why just to the library, then? Why not other places, or had she just not found *all* of the keys? But then why keep the library key on a separate ring? She shook her head, drowning in all the questions, and glanced around her to see what was in the room.

The room was bare, with a yellow-brown carpet like the rest of the library, and the walls were the same bland color, so they obviously weren't what caught her attention. What did steal her gaze was the stack of books slumped against the far wall, all of them having 'King Makero' and 'Queen Karenisha' written on them.

She rushed toward them and immediately began flipping through them, flicking through the pages using her tail. There were twelve in all. Each of them was lined with facts about the former King and Queen, and from the glimpses Saderia got of the words, they were all good things. She felt overjoyed that she had finally found something about her parents that did seem very reliable, but then she was confused. Why had they been in that room? Why had they been *hidden* in it?

Skimming them, they were all good things about all of her parents' great accomplishments as King and Queen, even if their time was short. There was information about the fire as well and the gist Saderia got from it was that it was as much of a big deal as she'd thought; five of the twelve hinted that it could have been set up. She wondered why anyone would hide these books, when they told everything about her parents and gave clues to the past…But with a sinking sense of unease, she couldn't deny what made the most sense.

Had someone purposely hidden them there to get rid of any traces of her parents, to let others wonder, or to try to make everyone forget the good they had done? For the five biographies, had they been hidden there to avert suspicion about the fire that had claimed their lives? The conversation with Dastarius still fresh in her mind, she felt even more horrified as she wondered why Cia had the keys to this door. As if *she* were the one who had hidden the books away for all those reasons.

Could Dastarius have been right? Were her aunt and uncle the ones who had started the fire to kill her parents, then made sure no one knew about it? She felt sick just thinking about it and a lump rose in her throat. No matter how they treated her, she cared about them and the thought that they could have done something so horrible, and lied and deceived her all those years was almost too much to bear. But she couldn't ignore what was in front of her. As her eyes began to grow misty with horror, she began to wonder about the other things they had done.

Whenever they went out to do something important that royalty should do, they had left her at home. They had discouraged her about her skills as a Queen, saying she wasn't ready and not giving any hint as to when she *would* be ready. And the Princess training they gave her was mindless and meaningless, not the kind of training that would prepare a Queen for her duty. Had they done that purposely to make her unfit to be Queen someday, because they wanted to rule the forest as long as they could?

As much as she wanted to, she couldn't just ignore her suspicions and how it seemed to make sense. She had to swallow hard to clear the thick lump in her throat. Had Cia and Jash really murdered her parents, and was she next?

Chapter Seven

Distrust

Saderia stayed in the room for a while, reading through the books and trying to figure out what she would do when she went home. She knew she would have to face Cia and Uncle Jash sometime.

Her thoughts were jumbled up and confused and she fought an impossible argument with herself. One part of her wanted to believe that Cia and Uncle Jash were the same animals she had grown up with knowing, and that they would never do something like that. That part of her said there was proof of their innocence in the things she had learned about them, and how they acted. Then again, another part of her argued that they were guilty, and they could have just been putting on an act the whole time. That part told her to watch her back and to pay close attention for new evidence.

She didn't know what to believe, but if her aunt and uncle *had* started the fire, they would pay. She didn't know how, but somehow she would make them regret what they did to them and to her, if it were true.

Only one thing was clear at that point: she couldn't do anything about it. *Yet*. She needed more proof in order to believe that Cia and Uncle Jash had done it, and she couldn't make her suspicions known to them in the meantime. Taking a deep breath, then slowly letting it out, she decided to act normal until she could distinguish between truth and suspicion. And she knew she had to go home sooner or later.

She crawled out of the room, setting the biographies back up against the wall. She was tempted to put them on the shelves, but if something were going on, she didn't want to arouse suspicion if the wrong animal found them there. With a heavy heart, she relocked the door and pushed the bookshelf back in place before leaving the library. A few animals said goodbye to her but she hardly noticed, walking down the dirt path to her house, her mind in a fog.

On the way home she tried to convince herself that it couldn't be true, but she couldn't help feeling suspicious. When she walked through the door to her house, she wasn't sure if she would be able to hold herself together. If what she suspected were true, then her whole life was a lie. How could she keep going, knowing that everything she had ever believed was wrong? Everything would be gone, and nothing would ever be the same.

For a moment she considered just forgetting about the whole thing, hoping that if she did then she wouldn't have to face any of it. But she knew she needed, above everything else, to know the truth. After finding out what she had, she needed answers more than anything, about what exactly had happened to her parents. If nothing else, she owed it to them to find out.

"Saderia, you're home! Did you find what you needed?"

Saderia jumped as Cia's voice drifted over to her and a moment later her aunt appeared from the hallway.

Cia walked over to her and frowned at her empty bag. Saderia froze, forgetting that she should have gotten a book to cover for the time she had taken.

"I, uh, I couldn't find the book I wanted," Saderia lied. "It was…checked out already."

"You didn't get something else then?"

"Um…no, because I had already wasted time looking for the book and I…wanted to get back."

"Why the rush?" Cia questioned, frowning at her.

"Because…" Saderia grasped for something, and finished lamely, "I have to finish my homework. I think I got a lot wrong and I want to finish before bedtime. I'm kind of slow sometimes, so I need the time."

Cia nodded, seeming to buy it. "Okay, if you need any help…"

"That's okay," Saderia said quickly, hurrying to get away from her.

She locked herself in her room and abruptly went to her bed, trying to calm herself down. That conversation hadn't been horrible or life-changing, she scolded herself, but she was so jumpy around them now. Letting out a weary sigh, she realized that even if she did drop it and let herself believe Cia and Uncle Jash were innocent, it could never be the same again. There would always be doubt.

Saderia stayed locked in her room for as long as she could, trying to sort out truth from theory. She looked through her mother's diary to try to find anything that might give her a hint about her aunt and uncle, but there was nothing particularly incriminating. But what was there didn't convince her they were innocent either. She dreaded the dinner call that would undoubtedly come, and when it did she had no choice but to leave her room and put on an act so her aunt and uncle wouldn't get suspicious.

When she bent over her food and said nothing after their attempts at conversation, Cia and Uncle Jash exchanged glances that Saderia wondered about. Were they worried about her, or worried about themselves?

Knowing she had to try to make conversation, she said the first thing she could think of. "How's the kidnapping case? Any leads?"

Cia shook her head. "No, and I don't think there will be. It's sad, but I think we're all out of options."

"That is sad," Saderia murmured appropriately, adding, "*I* know what that must feel like."

Cia gave her a hard look. "Saderia, we told you that we're not going to talk about this." *Ever*, was the word she didn't say, but Saderia could read it in her face.

"And why don't we talk about it?" she snapped. "You never tell me about them or about the fire. Don't you think I deserve to know?" She blurted it out without thinking but suddenly it became a clue against them. Why *hadn't* they ever said anything about it? Were they hiding something, and trying to get her to not look into it? Suddenly it seemed all too likely. A sense of danger made her instinctively unsheathe her claws. She really wanted to leave the table.

"You were too young to remember so why should we talk about it?" Cia snapped.

Saderia pushed her plate away. "I'm not hungry." She started to get up to walk away but Cia called her back.

"You weren't excused," she said frostily.

"Let her go," Uncle Jash argued. "It's just the three of us, so what's it matter?" Quieter he added, "Can't you see that she's upset?"

Cia cut her eyes at him but then nodded at Saderia. "Okay, you can go."

"Thanks, Uncle Jash," Saderia muttered, leaving the room.

As she walked, she wondered if they were guilty, and if they were, was it both of them or just one? Uncle Jash didn't seem like he would have done it, but then again, she couldn't really picture Cia doing something like it either. She wondered about it for the rest of the night until Cia called her to tell her it was time for bed.

Not bothering to read for another hour, Saderia turned out the lights and slumped on her bed with a weary sigh. Nothing was ever easy anymore; it felt like something inside her was being torn. Uncle Jash knocked on the door to say goodnight but Cia wasn't with him.

"Where's Cia?" Saderia asked, as he came over.

"She...can't understand," Uncle Jash replied after thinking about it for a while.

"Can't understand what?"

"Why you want to know so much about...your parents. After all, you were young..."

"Oh," Saderia muttered. "Tell her...the past matters as much as the future. At least, that's what I think."

"I could tell you..." Uncle Jash began but then shook his head. "Never mind. Sorry."

"Goodnight," Saderia replied, not meeting his gaze.

"Goodnight," he answered, walking out of the room. He paused at the door. "You are just like your mother," he murmured quietly, before closing the door softly.

Saderia's ears perked up and she stared at the door for a long time, before turning away and letting herself sink into sleep.

She was greeted by a rush of intense heat and the wails and shrieks of panicking animals. Right in front of her, a tree being devoured by evil flames cracked sickeningly and fell violently towards her. Terror made every inch of her body freeze and go numb as she awaited the inevitable. She couldn't move to get away from the falling tree and she knew that when it hit her, she was going to die.

But suddenly she was knocked away just as the tree smashed against the ground which exploded into flame. Although surrounded by a burning forest and smoke blacker than night, she somehow managed to look through the smoke and make out a face, but it was like looking at her reflection in a pool of water after a rainstorm.

"Mom?" she whispered. Saderia was barely aware of the fact that she couldn't control what she said and did. The words that escaped her were true to what she was feeling, but it was like she was reading a script, and not able to do anything else.

The face turned away from her to look somewhere else. She called something that Saderia couldn't make out through the darkness that was starting to cloud her mind. But then the tiger was over her again, whispering to her, "It's okay, Saderia, you're going to get through this. Just hold on!"

She felt like a baby again although she seemed to be the same age as she was when she had fallen asleep. None of this was real, she knew, but it felt like nothing she had ever experienced before. The feelings of fear and terror, then recognition and hope that were rushing through her now were as real as any she had ever felt. This scene had never happened in the past, it couldn't have, and yet it felt so real it frightened her.

In this strange and terrifying trance, it finally dawned on her just where exactly she was and she turned to the tiger frantically. "Mom, this is the fire!" she screeched, her throat closing on the words as smoke slammed into her lungs. The pain in her throat and the fumes from the smoke were exactly as they would be in real life and terror made her numb again as she wondered if maybe she had gotten it wrong, and this wasn't a dream. But she turned to her mother and rasped, "If you don't get out, you're going to die!"

The tiger, her mother, smiled weakly at her. "I know, Saderia, but I have to help my forest and I have to help *you*. Don't you know that's what being a Queen is all about? A good leader is someone who's not afraid for themselves but for others they care about. A true leader does whatever they can to know the truth, to help, to make a difference. When I'm gone, that will be your job."

"You can't go!" Saderia croaked. "You're not supposed to die, this was all set up!"

The tiger stepped backward into the flames surrounding them and for a moment, her orange fur was glowing in the flames instead of burning. Saderia gasped as her mother smiled at her and continued to back away.

"You're a true leader, you just don't know it," her mother whispered, the words too low to be heard but carried to Saderia's ears nonetheless. The fire roared, but Saderia didn't hear it at all; everything else faded away into the background so that the only thing that mattered was her and her mother.

"I'm not!" Saderia protested. "You have to stay, you have to help me!"

"Just hold on," her mother repeated, and then she disappeared into the fire, as Saderia woke up sobbing.

The next day, Saturday, was even worse for Saderia for several reasons. She hated Saturdays because her tutors didn't show up with homework and, even though she hated them and their teaching was boring, the homework they left gave her something to do all day. On top of that, she wanted to avoid Cia and Uncle Jash as much as possible until she knew more about what was going on. But on a Saturday, she had no helpful homework excuse. And her dream topped it off, making her wonder whether she should try to read a deeper meaning into it or just pass it off as any usual dream that occurred when she was upset about the fire. No matter what it was, it still distressed her, and that didn't make the day any easier.

But luck was with her because after Cia called her and she walked out, assuming breakfast was ready, Cia told her that they were out of food and she was going to the store.

"I'll go," Saderia offered quickly.

Cia frowned. "Really? That would be nice,

but..."

"It's no big deal," Saderia replied. "I'd be happy to. Just give me the list and I'll be back as soon as possible." A lie; she'd delay going back as much as she could, but she just smiled at Cia, hoping she would agree.

"Okay," Cia said, handing her a list. "Thanks."

"No problem," Saderia said, running out of the door as soon as she had gotten it.

She let out a sigh of relief when she hit the dirt path running, feeling the cool morning air flow through her fur. A light breeze ruffled the leaves on the trees and Saderia felt grateful and happy, as always, at being allowed outside. She loved the freedom of being able to run, tossing her cares aside and feeling nature welcome her warmly with open arms, like a mother would.

Letting her thoughts fly away, she let her paws carry her to her destination, feeling almost like she was flying. She nimbly dodged sharp stones on the path and roots sticking up through the dirt, wishing she could go on running like that forever. But she eventually reached the grocery store and began searching for the things she needed to get. It didn't take long and she promptly paid for it all, carrying the bags in her mouth and ignoring the exaggerated respect every animal in the store had to give her.

Heading back home, she let her paws drag unlike when she had run. She didn't want to have to go back and face all that she wanted to forget. All of the complicated things she had wanted to escape were back there. Briefly, she thought about running away, but that would just make things worse. A missing Princess was the last thing the forest needed to deal with and even if she was having problems at home, she owed it to her forest to see it through.

Thinking about that made her dream come back to her and the brief dream conversation she had had with her mother. The things she had said about what being a Queen and a leader meant swirled around in her mind, forcing her to think about it. Determination filled her as she realized that it *was* her duty now. Whether she was a Princess, a Queen, or one of the common animals, it didn't matter; she had to be a leader. It was true that she didn't really know how to be one yet, but with her mother's words ringing in her mind, she began to think that just maybe she could figure it out. On her own, as always.

She had to know the truth, for her sake as well as the forest's. If Cia and Jash really had done something, it was ultimately up to her to find out and make sure the forest was safe. Whatever her feelings about it were had to be put aside, although she knew already that that wouldn't be easy, if not impossible. As she walked along the dirt path, she felt the weight of what she had to do crushing her. Even though she knew what she should do, she still didn't want to go back. But she raised her head a little higher, trying to shut out those feelings and focus on the road ahead.

Walking through town was like walking over hot coals for Saderia. Lots of animals were there and they all felt that they had to pretend to worship the ground she walked on. Most of them clearly resented it but it was an unspoken rule and she couldn't do anything about it now. So she ignored it and kept on, trying to ignore the prickling of her fur as her appearance turned many heads and eyes bored into her back.

"Princess Saderia," a voice called out.

She would have ignored it, except that she knew that voice and she knew that tone.

She turned around and glared. "Are you following me?"

Dastarius stared back at her, undisturbed by her harsh words. "Following you? Why would I want to do that?"

"How should I know?" she replied. "What are you doing here anyway?"

"What do you think I'm doing here? This is the closest town." He smirked at her, amused. "You sound a little paranoid."

"I'm not paranoid," she snapped. "Just stressed. The life of royalty is tough, you know."

"It is," Dastarius agreed. He changed the subject and asked, "Have you found anything out about the fire?"

Saderia flinched, then looked around at all the

animals in the town. All of them were staring at them, not even bothering to hide the fact that they were watching them.

"Maybe here isn't the best place to talk," Dastarius said, following her gaze.

"You think?" Saderia replied, glaring at the animals.

She had no choice but to follow Dastarius as he led her away from the town into the trees, growling something she didn't catch to the closest animals. When they left, the animals all reluctantly returned to what they were doing. Saderia observed them through the trees, hissing to herself at the way they had stared at them so obviously, just because they were powerful and well-known in the forest.

Dastarius looked after them too. "Annoying, isn't it?" he commented. But when Saderia looked at him, he didn't seem too annoyed. More pleased than annoyed that he was so important to the other animals. "So have you found anything out?" he pressed.

"Not really," Saderia muttered. "I'm trying to find some stuff out about Cia and Jash."

"So you think it might have been them?"

Immediately defensive, she hissed, "I don't know! No, but it doesn't hurt to check! It's the only thing I've got to go on!"

"It was just a question," Dastarius responded, in a way that seemed like he was trying to hide a laugh.

"Why should I tell you this anyway?" Saderia

hissed, narrowing her eyes.

"Why shouldn't you?" he retorted, taking her off guard.

She could answer that, and yet she couldn't. She said nothing in the end and changed the subject by saying, "Have *you* found anything out?"

He shook his head. "Nothing more than what you have." He became serious. "You should consider Cia and Jash likely suspects. You can never be too careful."

"I guess," Saderia muttered. "I'm trying to find some kind of hint. I'll try to look out for anything that can tell me about what happened. I've already found some things from the past, so how hard can it be to find something else?"

"Maybe you're looking in the wrong place," he suggested, before walking off.

Saderia sighed and walked after him, back into town. By the time she got there, he was out of sight but she didn't really care about that. It was hard to summon back the courage she had felt before but she finally forced herself to be brave and go back to her home. However, the courage she had now was only a fraction of what it had been.

When Saderia arrived back at her house, she dropped the groceries off in the kitchen before withdrawing to her room, calling a hasty hello to her aunt and uncle. For the rest of the day, she sat there, wondering how she was going to find out anything if she stayed locked up in there all day.

She didn't have too many options, though. She went out of her room when breakfast, lunch and dinner were called but mainly just stayed inside, wishing she could be outside where it was freer.

Sunday passed pretty much the same and Saderia sat in her room all day, bored, waiting for something to happen. Nothing happened. She started to feel like she had years ago, when she was still small and hopeful. When she was young, she had waited, hoping her parents would somehow return to life to find her.

Monday was the same as Sunday, except Saderia had to sit through boring lectures but busied herself with as much homework as possible when it was over. Beginning to feel like she was getting back into her old life of an endless rut, she felt discouraged. She never wanted to go back to the tedium, and she needed to find out what had happened in the past, and what was going to happen as a result in the future.

By Tuesday, she was fed up with herself for letting herself start to fall back into what she had tried so hard to escape. She knew she wouldn't understand anything new if she just laid around waiting for it to come to her. She had to go to it. The best way to discover anything was to look for it.

So after dinner with her aunt and uncle, she rushed through her homework, hardly caring what she got right, and opened the window to sneak outside. She couldn't explore the house with Cia and Jash hanging around all day; that would have to wait for later. So the outside would have to do for now.

Saderia had no idea what exactly she was looking for, but she probably didn't need to. To discover something, she didn't have to know what she was trying to find, she just had to start looking. Reminding herself of this, she began nosing through the clumps of bushes around her yard, trying to pick up any hint. She was open to other clues but had a few things in mind for clues she could find from the fire: a still-standing charred tree, the skeleton of an old burned bush, maybe even a match that was never discovered. Any of those things might possibly have some sort of clue from the past.

She pawed through healthy green clumps of bushes, and noticed the natural brown of the tree trunks, supporting huge branches of light green leaves. She had hoped that there might be something left, even if it was so long ago, but it didn't look like it. The cool grass under paw was refreshing and carried none of the horror and terror that the fire had once brought ten years ago.

Gazing around at the peaceful trees, she felt disheartened, knowing there was probably nothing to find. With a sigh she started to head back to her window, but took the long way around the house, just in case. As she was rounding the corner a few paces from the house, her paw caught on something, and she looked down. Then she drew back with a gasp.

Right in front of her, previously hidden by a bush, were four old, faded cans. The grass had grown over them and they were dirty with age, but even in such a shape she could detect the harsh tang of gasoline.

Her heart began pounding so hard she thought her chest would explode as she hesitantly drew forward to look inside the gasoline tanks. All of them were empty; a bad feeling settled uncomfortably in her stomach. They looked old, as if they had been there for a very long time, and with a sharp gasp, she turned her back on it and darted back to her window to cower under her canopy.

She had obviously found a clue from the past, more than she could have ever hoped for. But she wished with all her heart that she hadn't. It was obvious she had found an incriminating clue but she wanted to believe that she was getting something wrong. She convinced herself that she still didn't have enough proof to decide one way or another.

Nonetheless, she couldn't stop a dark scene from enfolding in her mind. Cia and Jash had just laid a trail of gasoline to trap her parents then started the forest on fire. As planned, her parents ran out to try to stop it, as was their duty as King and Queen, but the trail they had laid spread and trapped them, killing them. They managed to finally put out the fire and then put on a show of fake sorrow when they discovered what had happened to the King and Queen. But then they took their titles and it was soon forgotten, except for the King and Queen's daughter, Saderia, and they made sure to keep her as much in the dark as they possibly could.

Saderia's claws tore the mattress beneath her but she hardly noticed the ripping sound. She hoped, for Cia and Jash's sake if not her own, that that hadn't happened, because she had never felt like she could ever kill anyone, but if they had done that, they would pay.

She squeezed her eyes shut to stop the tears that would surely come and took a deep breath, trying to calm herself. Still feeling alarmed, she began to wonder what would happen to her if she found out Cia and Jash *had* done it. It was obvious that she couldn't live with them anymore, so she'd have to become a runaway. She didn't have any friends or anyone to turn to so she would have no help.

Maybe she would have to…get rid of Cia and Jash for what they did, but then she'd be orphaned all over again. What would she do then? She was all out of options for where to go after that. Would she be *adopted*? How would that affect the royalty rules, though? By blood, she was to inherit the throne when she was twenty but she was only ten now, and if Cia and Jash had to be taken care of, who would rule the forest then? Certainly, she was too young, wasn't she? So then would the forest have to go without a King or Queen for *ten years*?

That was impossible, and the forest would have a very hard time dealing with such news and then the loss of a ruler for so long. So that was not an option. But what *would* happen if she found out that her aunt and uncle were...killers? They couldn't just go on ruling after what they'd done, could they?

Saderia's head ached from so much thinking and her heart hurt. Despite all those more important concerns, how would *she* cope if she learned that Cia and Jash really had started the fire, ended her parents' life, and ruined hers? She knew without a doubt, that she, nor anything else, would ever be the same again.

Tormented with what she might have to face, she buried her face in her pillow, and before she knew it, she was asleep.

Her dreams that night were as confusing as ever, to match her feelings. She felt pain, betrayal and fear swirling around in the black night of her dream vision, and the background was filled with the crackling of flames and intense heat, as all her dreams were centered around. Once she heard an animal cry out in pain, and then another time she heard an animal snarl, but it held no meaning in this dream except to induce terror.

And beneath all the other feelings and sounds, she could hear a noise from the background. A quiet voice was murmuring indistinctly but at times Saderia could pick out some words.

"The truth is never easy...but it must be found...keep going......"

The voice sounded as if it had come from the past, and it was speaking to itself, but in this dream it was as if the speaker were directing it at her. She *knew* the words were for her to hear, but she didn't want to listen. She didn't want this huge, ten-year burden placed squarely on her shoulders alone.

When she awoke, she gasped and made sure she was safely in her room. She noticed that the blanket had been pulled around her but she hadn't made it that way. Cia and Uncle Jash must have put it like that when they came in to say goodnight. With that thought, Saderia wanted desperately to believe they were innocent and just move on with her life, but she knew she couldn't now. She needed all the facts.

With a heavy sigh, she got up and went to the dining room when Cia called her, trying to act normal through breakfast. She sat through the horrible time with her tutors and zipped through her simple homework. Suddenly she was anxious to be outside and anxious to know what had happened. Not knowing was the worst torture to her now; knowing the truth became her top priority.

She didn't know how she could possibly get any more answers, though, so she stayed in her room and tried to think. After a while she thought that maybe she could talk to someone who had known her parents and her aunt and uncle pretty well and had worked with them sometimes. She could ask that animal how Cia and Jash acted toward her parents and ask in a subtle way if they might have seemed jealous and…plotting.

Fortunately, she knew of an animal that would know things like that. Unfortunately, that animal happened to be someone she least trusted, for reasons she couldn't quite understand. All the same, she had to at least try and see what information could be gathered from it. Without giving a chance to back down, she grabbed paper and a pen from her bedside table and made herself walk casually down the hallway to the front room. There she looked through one of the drawers until she found what she was looking for.

The King and Queen needed to have a lot of information about all the animals in their forest. She knew there were hundreds of records kept at one building, accessible only to them and the animals they described, but she didn't know how to get there and didn't need them anyway. In the house, they had a huge book filled with the addresses of all the forest animals and as Saderia flipped through it, she found the right animal and wrote the address down on the piece of paper. She put the book back and concealed the paper under her paw as she called, "Cia, Jash, I'm going to the library, okay?!"

"Okay, Saderia!" Cia called back. "Be back soon!"

"I will!" Saderia turned and raced for the front

door. Once she was outside, she glanced at the address and what part of the forest it was in, then took off running at top speed.

Dastarius's house actually wasn't that different from Saderia's house, from the outside at least. The house was placed in the middle of the woods with a path leading into town that was less trodden than the dirt path from Saderia's own house. There were no other houses within a few miles of it, being out in the middle of the woods instead of in one of the towns or neighborhoods. For those reasons, it had been very difficult to find but eventually she had gotten there.

She took a deep breath, standing on the edge of the clearing the house overlooked. She wasn't sure if she could get up the nerve to do this, and she suddenly felt young and afraid. But then she remembered her parents and her mother's pleading for her to find the truth. For her to be a true leader. She recalled her own need to know exactly what had happened. So after taking another deep breath, she marched forward.

The trees around her swayed and made creaking noises that seemed sinister for some reason. Other than the rustle of the trees, there wasn't a sound, but Saderia didn't let any of that faze her and kept her focus as she knocked on the door. Her heart pounded so fast it burned with pain but she made sure she didn't look as nervous as she felt as Dastarius answered the door.

His amber eyes widened when he saw her. "Princess?"

"It's Saderia," she replied coolly, trying to act serious but casual at the same time. It was not an easy thing to do.

He eyed her uncertainly, stepping out and shutting the door behind him with his black-tipped tail. "What are you doing here?"

Saderia felt a flicker of fright and almost turned and ran away but instead she was brave and calmly asked, "I want to talk. To ask you some questions about...before the fire."

"Ah." Dastarius seemed to understand. "So you're still trying to find out what happened."

"Yes."

"All right, ask me then."

Saderia wondered if he was having as tough a time trying to keep his composure as she was but dismissed that thought as she tried to get the rest of her thoughts straight.

"You were one of Karenisha and Makero's advisors..." she began, trying to figure out what to say. "So they had those meetings sometimes when they were Queen and King, right?"

Dastarius nodded.

"And you were there?" When he said yes, she went on, "And Cia and Jash? Were they there?"

"Yes," Dastarius told her, looking curious. "So you believe it was them?"

"I didn't say that!" she protested. "Aren't I supposed to be asking the questions?"

He smiled faintly in amusement. "Of course," he replied, as smooth as ever, "continue."

"Okay then." She sucked in a silent breath. "Well, did Karenisha and Makero control everything, or did Cia and Jash help, too?"

"Karenisha and Makero were the ones that were in charge. They were the ones every animal went to whenever they had a question or needed help. They were the ones that made the decisions and announced it to the forest. Cia and Jash did none of that, though they did help your parents to make *some* decisions."

"So..." She didn't want to have to say it but she had to. "So Karenisha and Makero were the ones with so much power over everyone else, and Cia and Jash had no power? No one really recognized them even when they did help make some decisions sometimes?"

"That's right."

"How did Karenisha and Makero accept their decisions?"

"Sometimes they took a few things from their suggestions to add to their plans, but it was obviously their ideas that were most important to the forest."

"Were Cia or Jash...well, did they seem...jealous or frustrated because of this?"

Dastarius's eyes gleamed. "I noticed something like that a few times. Cia seemed a little frustrated when one of her ideas wasn't accepted, or when she didn't really get the credit she might have deserved. And it wasn't too hard to see that sometimes they were jealous. The fight proved that, I suppose."

"What? Wait--what fight?"

"It was a few days before the fire," he explained. "Cia and Karenisha got into a big fight at one of the meetings because Cia accused Karenisha of taking all of the credit and control for herself. Claws were unsheathed."

Saderia shivered. "Were they really like that?" she blurted out. "They really kept all the control for themselves and acted...I don't know, selfish?"

"Slightly, but they were a new King and Queen. Some new Kings and Queens turn to others for help because they're overwhelmed. But some, like your parents, tend to try to get through the first, hardest part by just taking over and trying to get it straight. They make sure everyone knows they're in charge. Eventually they would have reached a point where it was more evened out...if they'd had a chance to get there."

Saderia wondered if this was the reason why the websites at the library had said such bad things about her parents. She must have been right that they just hadn't been given a chance to be known. Then what Dastarius had said about Cia and Karenisha fighting fully sunk in and a lump formed in her throat.

"Right before the fire?" she whispered.

"About three or four days before it," Dastarius

replied, knowing what she meant.

Saderia swallowed hard. "Okay."

He looked at her curiously. "Have you found anything else that might make you suspect them?"

Saderia looked at him for a long moment then looked down. "Gasoline," she muttered finally. "Four old, empty tanks that used to have it."

Dastarius looked stunned. "That *is* disturbing."

Saderia nodded absently. "I need to get back. I have to think about something."

"Of course."

Saderia turned around and stalked away, keeping her eyes on the ground. As soon as she heard the door shut, she took off running in the direction of town, remembering her lie and deciding to back it up this time. After checking out a few books at the library just to give herself an alibi, she then raced back to her house.

"I'm back," she called, half-heartedly. It was just a natural response and she rushed to her room without waiting for a reply. She had been right; her whole world was starting to crumble apart. Even if she didn't completely trust Dastarius, what he had said had seemed like the truth but it also seemed scary. Given the other evidence and likeliness, it was incriminating. And she didn't know what to do.

She curled up under her canopy bed with her mother's diary and let tears streak down her face. What she wouldn't give right then to have her normal life back, no matter how boring. At least she didn't hurt as much back then. At least she knew what was what back then. But there was no going back.

She didn't leave her room or the position she was in, and somehow Cia and Jash, her possibly murderous aunt and uncle, knew better than to try to disturb her when she didn't answer to their mealtime calls. She knew it wasn't doing her any good to starve but that didn't matter to her. All that mattered was that everything she had grown up with knowing was starting to come apart.

The next day she stayed cooped up in her room again. She hadn't slept well that night, too scared to close her eyes when Cia and Jash were just feet away. That day she came out only to grab breakfast and take it back to her room. She couldn't face her aunt and uncle when her suspicions about them were so high. It still terrified her to think of what she might have to do when she finally found the right evidence to prove they were guilty. She had enough right now to believe it in her own mind, but she needed more if she wanted to prove something. But she was scared to look for more, or get any help. Besides, who could she turn to anyway?

Her tutors had to come to her room and they complained that she was distracted and not paying attention. They didn't know the half of it. Eventually they learned that they should just go on with their lessons and pretend like she cared. Like her, they should pretend they were doing what they were supposed to, and leave well enough alone. Finally they left and Saderia just stared at the homework they had left. What did homework matter when everything else was falling apart? She threw the stack of it against the wall where it exploded into a flurry of disturbed papers. She didn't bother to pick it up, just laid back on her bed with troubled eyes.

Friday was the same way and Saderia was almost afraid to leave her room. If she did, she might have to face the real world and she didn't know if she was ready for that. Sitting through her boring day, again she wondered what she would do. At the end, she stared at her math homework and didn't see the normal frustrating word problems, but different, more troubling problems, ones that said: *If a fire is spreading at 10 miles per hour, how much of the forest will be burnt down in 5 hours? How many homes will be destroyed? How many animals killed?* or, *If cans of gasoline are found five feet from a house, what is the probability that someone who lived there started the fire? Add to it an animal who knew them that is about 25% trustworthy, and then what is the probability?*

Saderia shoved the homework away from her and laid on her bed. There were no answers to any of those excruciating questions. She thought over everything she had found out about her parents, about the fire, Queen Tarae, the dungeon, the keys...everything and it was still not enough. She sat there contemplating what she could possibly do when she felt her stomach rumble at dinnertime; she had not had lunch.

Taking a deep breath, she opened the door to attempt to walk down to the dining room, using every bit of strength she had to act normal, but stopped when she saw what was behind her door. A dinner plate with her favorite foods lay there and she picked it up gingerly, going back in her room. On any ordinary day, it would have seemed like a nice gesture but now she wondered if that was what it was, or if Cia and Jash just didn't want her to come out. Maybe they wanted to keep her in her room forever, in the dark like they wanted. Or maybe they just wanted her to keep believing they were the nice animals they had always let on to be...or pretended to be.

She sighed, refusing to think about it. Whatever their reason, she had food and hadn't had to leave her room, so why complain? She chewed the food, laying on her bed, but it was hard to swallow and tasted like plastic. She stayed there for the rest of the night, then decided she should go out to put the plate up and maybe thank her aunt and uncle if they were there. And try to find out if there was something else going on.

She slunk out of her room, down the hall, through the dark front room and was about to creep into the dining room when she heard Cia and

Jash's voice from the living room. Frowning, she peered around the dining room arch to look through the arch to the living room. Cia and Jash were on the couch and she couldn't see them well because of the darkness but they didn't notice her either.

"Calm down," Uncle Jash was saying. "We've got plenty of time."

"Not enough time," Cia retorted.

"Ten years?" Uncle Jash replied. "Come on, it's not that urgent. Give it time."

"No," Cia hissed, and Saderia swore her tone was vindictive and angry. "Saderia *cannot* be Queen now or ever!" Uncle Jash muttered something inaudible. Then quieter Cia added, "I'll make sure of that."

"Cia…" Jash began but he broke off as a plate clattered to the ground and broke.

Both of them whipped around to see Saderia standing in the archway, the plate she had been carrying dropped, her amber eyes round with horror.

Cia got to her paws. "Saderia…"

But Saderia didn't wait to hear it. She whirled around and bolted to her room as fast as she could, forgetting the broken plate and everything else. Using her tail to slam the door behind her, she finally gave the vanity a good use by pushing it against the door as a blockade. Tears of fear and betrayal pricked her eyes and she took a few gasping breaths, trying to work out some logical explanation for what she had heard. There was none.

"Is *that* enough evidence?" she whispered hoarsely to herself.

Were Cia and Jash really planning to get rid of her? That was what it had sounded like to her, and her heart pounded with terror and the horrible ache of treachery. She couldn't just ignore everything else she had seen and found, and there was no more time to think. The only time she had to act was *now*.

For a moment she thought she would melt into a puddle of terror but then she sucked in a quick breath and forced herself to calm down. No matter what happened, she had to get through it and be strong. Her heart slowed and an eerie calm spread throughout her body to the ends of her limbs. Then, as soon as it had come, it was replaced by a burning anger. Saderia narrowed her eyes and took deep breaths before shoving the vanity aside and stomping out of her room.

Cia and Jash were in the front room, staring down at her hallway with fear and confusion in their blue eyes. Saderia hardly noticed it as she ran up to them, the fur on her back rising as a growl escaped from her throat.

"Saderia, what's wrong with you?" Cia exclaimed.

"What's *wrong* with me?!" Saderia exploded. "I'm sick of this! I'm sick of this life! I'm sick of the secrets! I'm sick of *you*!"

Cia's fur immediately fluffed out and she glared at Saderia. "What are you talking about?"

"The stupid life you make me live is just a ploy to keep me in the dark!" Saderia shouted. "I'm not a Princess-in-training, I'm an idiot-in-training! You've never listened to me about what I want and what I need! I wondered why before but it all makes sense now! You've kept secrets from me! Do you think I haven't found out about the secret compartment in your closet or Mom's store room or the dungeon?!" Cia's eyes went wild and she took a step back. Saderia continued savagely, "Or the room in the library, where you hid all the books about my parents so no one would know! So you could get away with it!"

"Get away with what?" Cia managed to get in. "How dare you yell at me like this?"

"How dare you act like you don't know?!" Saderia screamed. "What about the websites? Did you make those too?! Are you the one that put that horrible stuff on there about them and about the fire being 'no big deal?!'"

"I don't…!"

Saderia interrupted her, "Fine, play ignorant with that! But how do you explain the old gasoline tanks right outside this house?!"

Cia gasped. "Gasoline?! How…?" Then her eyes widened. "You think I…!"

"Shut up!" Saderia shouted. "Why don't you listen for once instead of pleasing yourself with hearing your own voice?!" She hissed. "It all adds up now! It all makes sense! How could you do that?!"

Cia glared at her. "You're way out of line!" she shouted back. "How dare you accuse me of this?! And you accuse *me* of keeping secrets when you clearly have some of your own?!"

"That's right, and I'm glad I never told you them either!" Saderia shouted.

Jash's eyes followed them as they spoke; he looked alarmed, horrified, confused and terrified all at the same time and didn't dare say a word.

"Your worse than your mother!" Cia screamed. "You don't know anything! You don't know what you're talking about so keep your mouth shut!"

"Don't you dare talk about my Mom! And you aren't telling me what to do anymore!"

"Fine, I won't talk about Karenisha, I'll talk about you!" Cia retorted, her eyes flaming but alarmed and scared. "If she were still alive, she'd be disappointed! You'll never live up to her expectations and you're nothing like what she would have wanted! You have no idea what you're talking about! You are making a fool of yourself and you're no Princess!"

"Fine, I'm glad I'm not!" Saderia screamed. "And I can't live up to her expectations because I can't live at all here! I've been dead for ten years because I certainly haven't lived those years! Because of you I'm no better than an inanimate object!"

Cia hissed. "Get to your room! You don't know what you're talking about!"

"I know exactly what I'm talking about! More than you think! And I don't have to go back to my room and be miserable for another ten years!" Saderia shook her head in disgust and rage. "This isn't even about me! This is about my parents and what *you* did! How could you?!"

"How could I *what*?" Cia snapped.

Saderia snarled. "Because of you, they're dead!"

"What are you talking about?" Cia shouted back. "You don't know anything!"

Saderia opened her mouth to say something but nothing came out. This was it. It all came to this. She staggered back a pace and blinked quickly to try to hold herself together. "You killed my parents," she whispered.

Cia drew back. *"What*?!"

"You killed my parents!" Saderia screamed as loud as she could.

She didn't wait to see what they would say to that. She whipped around unhesitatingly and raced out of the house and into the night as fast as she could. She didn't look back as tears began to slide down her cheeks. It would be too painful to see everything she had ever known disappear behind her.

Chapter Eight

Runaway

Saderia ran away from the house and everything she had ever known, her paws thudding on the dirt path. She veered off to try to run through the woods and stay hidden, but stumbled on the slope leading down to the more wooded part and ended up tumbling headfirst into the woods. Tears and mud streaked her face and body but she got up and kept running.

She didn't know where she was going and didn't have time to stop and think about it. But she didn't care; she just had to get away. Her paws tripped over roots and bushes, sharp stones and branches cut into her, but she didn't notice except to wince in pain. Her ear snagged on a sharp branch but she tore it free, ignoring the sting and kept moving. A fallen tree was in her way but when she tried to jump over it, her back legs hit it hard and she fell face-first into the dirt.

Sobs finally wrenched out of her throat, held back before only by the exhilaration of running and panting. When she tried to pull herself up she noticed the bottoms of her paws were bloody and cuts lined her face, back, sides, legs and tail. She let herself lay there for a while, trying to get her breathing under control, then finally picked herself up and kept running, the need to get away driving her to keep moving even though it was hard.

She didn't know if Cia or Jash would come after her, or if they would be glad she was gone. She just didn't know. Flicking leaves and brambles away from her with her tail, she kept moving through the woods, desperate to be anywhere but near the house where everything she had known was a lie. Struggling to keep moving, she tugged free of prickly bushes, vines and sharp sticks. But eventually she couldn't fight off exhaustion anymore and collapsed on the ground, instantly unconscious.

Her dreams made no sense after that. She was in a dark, dank place that she had never been before and she could see nothing around her. Very quietly, she heard a voice murmuring her name but couldn't make out what it was saying. A flash of betrayal sliced through her and she felt a rush of terror but suddenly she was in a different place although it was just as dark. If not for a sort of dream sense, she wouldn't have known she had switched places. Then suddenly a fire flickered to life in front of her. She panicked but then realized it was only a torch. A few feet in front of her was a scroll, and she could see nothing else. At that moment, the scene faded rapidly and she woke with a squeak of alarm.

For a moment she couldn't remember where she was but then last night's events came flooding back to her and she let out a cry of grief and sadness. She thought back to everything her aunt and uncle had done and what she suspected. She wanted to at least have good memories of them but everyone was tinged with betrayal.

She didn't know where she would be able to go; fear and confusion sunk sharp claws into her. Everything was happening right at that moment and she didn't have time to think about it. A tsunami of terror, horror and confusion crashed over her and she curled up in a ball, hoping to stay there forever.

She could have stayed there for a few moments or a few hours, but eventually she uncurled with a strange new sense of determination. Maybe she didn't know all the answers then, but she could figure them out. But that was still easier said than done.

Taking a deep breath, she tried to figure out a way to get all of her thoughts together and find a way to get through the ordeal. She forced herself to stop panicking and think clearly which eventually helped her heart slow and allowed her to breathe normally. The panic attack averted, she realized that if she looked at each thing she had to do one at a time, she might be able to figure out *something*.

So she forced her mind to center on one thought, her first and most pressing problem: where was she going to live? Although it scared her, she realized that living in the woods wouldn't be so bad. She liked it out there and she was free out there, so it couldn't be too awful. How long she stayed there was another question, but she was going to think of it as a permanent residence for the moment, seeing as she had no other options.

The next question was what to do about Cia and Jash. Once she figured out how she was going to live in the woods, in which particular place and how to survive, she could try to get help. She could use the evidence she had found and maybe look for more without being seen. Then maybe something would happen to them.

But then what would happen if there were no King and Queen? It was a possibility that Saderia could take over even if she was young, because the forest needed a ruler. But maybe she would have to let Cia and Jash rule for the next ten years. The thought angered her that they should get away with it but perhaps there was no other choice.

She didn't have to worry about that one for a while, she guessed, so she pushed it out of her mind. She wouldn't act until she knew more about what would happen and what she could do. Every action had a consequence.

She wondered if Cia and Jash were looking for her or just letting her disappear. Needing to find out, she planned to sneak through the woods as close to a town as she could get and look around, to see if they seemed to be panicked about a Princess going missing. Being careful, she judged where she was then set off in the direction of the nearest town. When she got closer, she walked more carefully, determined not to make a disturbance that would alert the animals to her presence.

When she peered through the bushes on the outskirts of town, she noticed animals running around frantically and a few posters were put up, announcing her absence. So Cia and Jash were going to play innocent, it looked like. Saderia let out a quiet sigh then squinted her eyes to study one of the posters. With a burning surge of fury she realized she was denounced a runaway. She was, it was true, but not because she was just some troubled kid who left home. Then she realized that the animals were worried and looking for her but also disappointed and disapproving. The title 'runaway' was all she was to them now, just a spoiled Princess who didn't get her way and so left home to punish her respectable aunt and uncle.

Saderia gritted her teeth to hold back an outraged hiss. To them, she was just a cause for concern and they were all angry at her for what it seemed like she had done. She wouldn't have gone to such measures as this if there were any other way, but no one knew that. Bitter, she stalked away from the town, back into the woods with her head and tail drooping.

When she pushed through a bush and saw brown paws beneath her, her head shot up and she jumped, letting out a shrill squeak of surprise. Her surprise quickly changed to fear which changed just as instantly to anger. Hoping no one else had heard her squeak she glared at the lion.

"What are you doing out here, Dastarius?" she hissed. "You're the last animal I want to see right now!" That wasn't true, but she was furious about her complicated, fake life and fed up with how others saw her. She just wanted to be alone.

Dastarius stood in front of her in the woods. Saderia was sure no one had heard her and no one was coming to find her. That, at least, was a relief but what would Dastarius do now that he found her?

He actually seemed amused at her reaction. "Having problems, Princess?"

"'Problems!'" she hissed. "After all that's happened I'd hardly call them something as simple as 'problems!' And don't say it like that! My whole life has just changed completely and I'm apparently a stupid runaway Princess now! My whole pathetic life has been destroyed! I slept in the woods last night, I have no idea what I'm going to do about Cia and Jash and if anybody will believe anything I say now that they think I'm just a spoiled runaway! So, yeah, I guess you could say I have 'problems!'"

Dastarius looked surprised. "Calm down," he told her. "One thing at a time."

"I suppose you're going to turn me over to Cia and Jash as the big hero who found the stuck-up Princess now," Saderia snapped, ignoring him.

"Not if you don't want to be found," he replied, surprising her.

Saderia blinked, thrown off guard. "What are you going to do then?" she asked cautiously.

"Whatever needs to be done. Why don't you start by telling me what you're doing out here and why you don't want to go back to Cia and Jash?"

"Because they're killers!" she burst out, without thinking.

Immediately serious, Dastarius said gravely, "So you finally found out for sure."

Saderia nodded miserably. "It has to have been them that started the fire. I...there were cans of gasoline outside of the house, and they were jealous of my parents, I guess, and I heard them talking about getting rid of me!" She shook her head. "Everything's so complicated! I...I don't know what to do!"

"They were talking about getting *rid* of you?" Dastarius sounded shocked. "When?"

"Last night. I ran...away...to my room, then I went back out and fought with them. I...accused them of killing my parents and Cia...she did it..." Saderia hadn't realized she was sobbing until then but she was, quietly. She realized how muddy and scratched up she looked and her sides shook with more tears. She hated how she was falling apart right in front of him and put a paw to her face, gripping her forehead and trying to blink back the tears. Her breathing was uneven as she choked out, "How could she...do that? How...how could they kill...my parents? Cia and my Mom...were sisters...twins!"

Dastarius was silent, watching her closely. Saderia drew in a deep choking breath, letting it out shakily. "I ran away after that. I passed out in the woods…I was running so fast…And I tried so hard to find out about the past…and now I don't want to know!" She took a breath to steady herself. "Now they're just…setting up this, this *stupid charade*! They made everyone think…I ran away because…" She let out a gasp as tears pricked her eyes and tried to swallow back the anger rising like bile in her throat. "Because I'm just some snooty, stuck-up Princess!" she practically screamed. "That's all I am to everyone else!"

Slowly, Dastarius nodded, taking it in and waiting for her to continue.

"I don't know what I'm supposed to do now!" she went on shakily. "Or where I'm supposed to go! Do I…do I just live out in the woods forever? Am I…supposed to just disappear? To just let them…get away with it?" She shook her head and swiped a paw across her face to brush the tears and dirt away but left a faint trail of blood instead.

Dastarius's black-tipped tail flicked the blood off her face and Saderia turned away.

"Why am I even telling you any of this?" she asked quietly, finally getting control of herself.

"You don't trust me." It wasn't a question.

"No," she answered anyway.

"Well, this is a situation where that really doesn't matter. I've given you no reason to distrust me, and you've got nowhere else to turn now, have you?"

"I guess not," she muttered. "You're not going to turn me in to them?"

He was silent for a long time. "No," he said at last. He went on, "The other animals have no idea what's going on. None of them would understand, not with Cia and Jash's *charade*. I think you're out of options, Princess."

"Tell me something I don't know!" she shouted, looking down again.

"Well, there are always new options. You could come stay at my home, for instance."

She looked up in shock and disbelief. "What?"

"It's better than the woods, I would think," Dastarius told her, taking in the streaks of dirt and scratches all over her.

"Well, I guess, but…"

"It won't be easy for you to do something to stop Cia and Jash on your own, you know. You're too young, and I'm sure you've already thought of all the consequences that could come if they were to…stop living."

Saderia flicked her ears. "Yes, I have. They're the only royalty left, besides me, and I'm only ten."

Dastarius nodded. "I'm not royalty, but I do have a lot of say as far as ruling the forest. I could help you do something about Cia and Jash, then sort out the complications afterward."

Saderia studied him closely. "But why would you help me?"

"It's my forest as well as yours, isn't it?"

"I suppose," Saderia murmured thoughtfully. What he said did make some sort of sense and it would be nice to have help in this tough situation. And he really *hadn't* shown any reasons for her distrust.

"You would only have to stay there until I've figured out a way to fix this," Dastarius went on. "Once it's been taken care of, you can go back to living in your home, and then become Queen ten years from now, as you were supposed to. You won't have to worry anymore."

That sounded very appealing to her, and she did kind of like the idea. It made her a bit uncomfortable but it seemed all right. Then she had another thought. "What about Cia and Jash?"

"I don't know what I'm going to do about them yet."

"No, I mean, what if they find out I'm staying at your house? What'll they do to you?"

"They won't find out," Dastarius replied. Seeing her skeptical look, he added, "And if they do, they're supposed to trust me and think I was just helping out. Or I could convince them I'd just found you that day."

"Maybe," Saderia muttered.

"I'll deal with them before then," Dastarius told her. "Besides, I don't think they'll find you. They're probably not even looking for you since, like you said, they're setting this up to make you look bad.

They might just be doing it for the publicity, and so no one will believe you, meanwhile they go on ruling as always."

His words hurt, but Saderia couldn't help but think he was right.

"Okay," she said, a little uncertainly, ignoring the strongly uncomfortable feeling that almost made her feel sick. "If you think this will work..."

"It will," he said, the hint of a smile on his face, though as usual, on his face it looked more like a sneer. "Let's go."

Brushing his tufted tail gently across her forehead to wipe away the dirt, surprising her, and then waving his tail as a sign for her to follow him, Dastarius led her through the woods in the direction of his house. They took a route that Saderia hadn't known about and after a few turns, she was even more lost than ever. She hoped Dastarius knew where he was going. He did, as it turned out, because they soon stumbled into the clearing where his house was located.

Saderia hung behind a little uncertainly then followed Dastarius through the door. She didn't really know what to expect on the inside but when she stepped through the door, it opened up into a living room. That first room looked pretty normal and maybe even welcoming so she began to relax slightly, wondering if she would be able to get used to it during her stay. A few faded couches were at one corner and a table with a computer was on another wall, a little like her house's front room.

On the right wall, there was an archway that led to a small hallway that veered to the left. Right across from the arch was another arch that led into a dining room. The table wasn't gold like in Saderia's house but it was just as rich-looking as in her house. There was an archway on the north wall of the dining room leading into the hallway that went far on the left, leading to a few different rooms. At the end of the hallway was a door but it appeared to be locked. Across from the dining room was the kitchen that looked as normal as any, and on the north wall of the kitchen was a door that opened to a screened porch.

"Nice house," she commented, suddenly aware of how ratty she looked.

Dastarius nodded absently then seemed to sense her discomfort. "The bathroom's the third door," he informed her, fighting a grin.

"Thanks," Saderia muttered, walking down the hall to the third door. She briskly hopped into the big shower and nosed the faucet to let water clean the dirt off of her. The scratches stung just slightly, but she ignored them since they had stopped bleeding. She shook her fur out and hastily walked back out to find Dastarius.

But when she didn't see him at first she slowly looked at the locked door at the end of the hall with strong curiosity. Slowly, she padded toward it and tugged on the knob, but it was still locked very tightly; she wondered, almost with an edge of desperation, what was behind it. But it was none of her business, so she walked away from it and back toward the living room where Dastarius was waiting.

"So...um, I could just sleep on the couch or something," Saderia suggested, not wanting to be a nuisance.

"If you want," Dastarius said. "The first door in the hall is my room, the second is the closet, and you've seen the rest of the house. Make yourself comfortable. I have to go."

"Where?"

"Out," he replied, flicking his ears. "Just something I need to look into. I'll be gone for a while."

"Okay..."

Without another word, he walked out the door, leaving her behind in the house. Saderia went to leap onto one of the couches, unsure of what to do. It seemed very strange to be staying at someone else's house since she had never had a reason to before. She had never been to anyone else's house now that she thought about it, because she didn't have any friends. Before, she had just been expected to stay at home, go outside on occasion, and follow Cia and Jash to wherever they brought her. In a way it felt good to be free of them but it also felt strange and a little scary. There was sorrow too, because she had loved her aunt and uncle no matter what; the pain of their betrayal still ached horribly. But then, this was what she had always wanted, right? To be free?

She thought about all that she had lost for a

while, and what she could possibly do to get revenge on Cia and Jash despite the sadness it
brought. But it was too hard and painful to think
about. So she used the time she had to think about
how long she was going to stay at Dastarius's
house and if she would be able to get used to it
somehow. She wondered what she would do now
that she had more freedom. Maybe she could even
be like a normal tiger once all this was over.

Eventually she grew hungry, having not eaten
since yesterday at dinner, and debated whether she
should get something from the kitchen. Finally telling herself that if she were to stay there, she might
as well get used to it and stop feeling so awkward
and out-of-place, she went to the kitchen to grab a
quick snack.

By that time it was getting to be night and she
couldn't help but start thinking about her parents
again, and how much she wished they were there
to help her. That was impossible, she knew, but
then she remembered her mother's diary. She had
left it behind. That, along with the ring of keys and
the things in her bedside table drawer that she treasured.

For a bit longer she thought about the things
she had left behind when she had run out so fast.
She felt as if she *had* to get them, and knew she
would definitely miss them. All of it was important
to her and she didn't want to lose it when she felt
so lost herself. Something besides her need to get

her treasures was telling her she had to go back to that house, so she finally made a plan. Tonight, she would sneak over to her old house, sneak into her bedroom window, take her things, then go back to Dastarius's house. She could probably find the way. Dastarius hadn't been back yet, and it would probably be a while before he returned, so he wouldn't even miss her absence.

Dastarius hadn't locked the door so she snuck out of it easily, not having to worry about that. Her eyes quickly adjusted to the darkness of the forest and she took off running, more agilely this time because now she had a destination and a purpose, unlike when she had run away. The peaceful noise of crickets making their nighttime songs soothed her as she moved through the forest, using bushes for shelter. Her amber eyes glowed in the dim light as she made her way back through the forest. The cool night air was refreshing and gentle against her scratches. Leaping over sharp rocks and dodging trees, again she felt as if she belonged there and could go on forever like that. But when she finally saw her old home through the trees, she was jolted back to the current situation and slowed down to creep along more stealthily.

She crept over to her bedroom window and carefully nosed it open. Crawling through the small space, she gingerly stepped into her old bedroom, feeling equal waves of sadness and contempt wash over her. She missed her old sanctuary and the way things used to be; there was no denying it. But at the same time she was glad that that was behind her, that she had more freedom, that she wasn't expected to put on an act all hours of every day.

Reminding herself that there was no time for this, that she should just get what she came for and run, she stepped over to her bedside table and carefully slid the drawer open, feeling a wave of déjà vu. How many times before had she opened that drawer, seeking comfort from the diary and the other things? Gingerly, she picked up her mother's diary and the other things she kept it her drawer. She couldn't find the ring of keys and with a stab of anger she realized Cia and Jash must have raided her room and found them. Why hadn't they taken the diary, then? She shook her head, not caring. The keys weren't *that* important anyway; she could live without them.

Turning around to leave through the window, she suddenly heard a sound from outside, sort of a thundering of paws, as if many animals were running together. It made the orange fur along her back stand up. Yells and snarls sounded from outside and fear spiked through her entire body. At the same moment an awful banging sound came from the front room, like something ramming on the door. What was going on?

Frozen to the spot, she wasn't sure whether to run out when all that horrible noise was coming from outside, or retreat into the house, where Cia and Jash were. It turned out she didn't have to make a decision because at that moment, Cia and Jash burst into the room and froze.

"Saderia!" Cia gasped.

Saderia backed up against the wall, letting out a fearful hiss. "Get away from me!"

"Saderia, you don't understand!" Cia begged, taking a step toward her. "I…"

Jash let out a terrified, frustrated hiss. "There's no time for this! Where's the key?!"

Feeling very confused, Saderia's gaze was instantly drawn to a key laying on the floor by her bedside table. It must have fallen off the ring of keys when Cia had taken them and she hadn't noticed. Cia saw it too and grabbed it. "Hurry!" she exclaimed, rushing toward Saderia.

Saderia didn't move fast enough to run away and Cia grabbed her scruff with her teeth, making her drop what she had gotten. Cia tugged her along without waiting for her consent and the best Saderia could do was to use her tail to push her treasured belongings under the bed where they might be safe. There was still the sound of shrieking outside and a few growls.

"What's going on?" Saderia demanded, trembling. "Stop pulling me!"

"Then walk on your own and keep your voice down!" Cia snapped, letting go of her but shoving her through the dining room. Both of them looked very scared and confused; Saderia couldn't make sense of any of it. She didn't know whether to be afraid of them or afraid of what was going on outside but she didn't have much choice.

They reached the living room and Jash shoved up against one of the couches, pushing it aside, revealing an old, rusted trap door. Saderia's eyes widened and her mouth opened in wonder.

"A trap--"

She was cut off by Cia hissing at her to be quiet and she watched as her aunt pushed the key into the lock on the trap door. So *that* was where the last key went! Jash used a paw to haul it open with a loud creak and Cia briskly pushed Saderia inside. She almost stumbled down a long, dirty flight of stairs, just barely catching herself. Cia joined her inside and Jash pulled the couch over the trap door, closed it, locked it, then rushed down to them. Both of them pulled Saderia down the long, dark stairs into a pitch black, dank, old, tiny room.

The tiny, underground room was sort of like a cellar, but once inside, Cia and Jash held Saderia there and instructed her to be very quiet.

"What's going on?" she demanded anyway.

Cia's blue eyes were wide with fear. "I don't know," she whispered.

"Something very bad," Jash hissed.

For the first time her aunt turned to really look at her. "You came back," she said softly.

"And what great timing," Jash growled, but he looked more afraid for her than angry.

"I just came back to get my stuff," Saderia snapped. "Why are we down here?"

"Protection," Cia told her. "Saderia, don't you understand? We're in danger!"

Saderia opened her mouth to speak but closed it again, fear shivering up her spine.

Cia's face was creased with pain. "How could you ever think that we could have ...could have killed...?" She trailed off, deeply hurt.

"What else am I supposed to think?" Saderia shouted. "All the evidence is against you! It makes sense!"

"What evidence?"

Suddenly the growls were much closer and panic shot up her spine as Saderia realized that something was in the house...searching for them.

"What's going on?" she hissed, her voice shaking with fear.

"We're being attacked," Cia whispered, her eyes wide with panic.

"A-attacked?"

"Maybe by who started the fire," Jash said gravely. "If you say you have evidence that that happened."

Saderia's head was whirling. Had she made a really bad mistake? If Cia and Jash hadn't killed her parents, then who had? And what were they going to do now? Who were their attackers? Then she heard a terrible noise: the sound of furniture being turned over.

"They're going to find the trap door!" she exclaimed.

The color drained out of Cia and Jash's faces

and they turned to look at each other, as if wondering what to do. What could they possibly do? They were trapped.

Suddenly the sound of wood splintering cut through the air and Saderia let out a little shriek. "What do we do?"

Neither Cia nor Jash had an answer and all they could do was sit there helplessly, waiting for their attackers to find them. What did they want anyway? Saderia wondered as terror and utter confusion clouded her mind. Then she felt a pang of pain and anger at herself as she realized that maybe she had been wrong about Cia and Jash. She wasn't completely sure either way, having no concept of what was going on, but it made her feel horrible for running away when she might have been wrong.

But she had other, scarier things to worry about at that moment, because a loud, hideous crack sounded from above them. In a matter of seconds a mob of animals poured down into their tiny, underground hiding place. Saderia let out a shriek when she saw the first of them and tried to hiss warningly while Cia and Jash backed against the wall, preparing to fight even though it was hopeless.

When Saderia saw the collection of animals that stopped to confront them, at first she saw only a mass of outraged, evil animals, but at second glance, she saw something more. These animals were hungry and dirty, and a gleam of desperation, dulled by some sort of grief, shown in their eyes. There was hope in them but mostly anger at Cia, Jash and Saderia. But she could tell that there was more to them than just a bunch of cruel attackers. All the same, the situation was just as terrifying and the desperation about them inspired even more fear; sometimes when someone was desperate, they'd do anything.

Beside her, Cia let out a gasp. "What is the meaning of this?" she demanded.

A panther stepped forward, desperation and grief rolling off of him in waves. "We're sick of you controlling things," he growled. "You never help anybody. You can't help us and you can't help the forest."

"Call yourself a King and Queen?" another animal snarled.

"We're trying…" Jash began, only to be cut off by the panther.

"No, you're not, you gave up. You stopped caring. A better King and Queen wouldn't."

"What are you going to do with us?" Saderia demanded, hating the way her voice gave away her fear. She tried to prepare herself for a fight but she could already tell that it wouldn't end well.

"What we were told," one of the animals muttered.

Saderia didn't know what that meant but it sent shivers up her spine. Was someone else controlling them and telling them to do this? Could it be the same animal that had started the fire ten years ago?

She didn't have long to think about it because, without warning, the animals sprang at them and shoved them against the wall. Saderia let out a furious hiss and scratched at them with her claws, snapping with her fangs whenever any of them came close enough. She couldn't see Cia and Jash since she was cornered by a swarm of animals but could guess they were being attacked just as brutally.

Suddenly a blow to her back from behind caught her off guard and she went sprawling forward. A panther and a lion pounced her to the ground and she struggled to throw them off. But it was no use because soon the other animals advanced on her. All she could do was dodge the claws raking her fur and the powerful blows but when she was distracted in fending off another side, an unexpected blow struck her hard on the head. She let out a roar of pain and fell toward the wall. An animal snapped her head back and she was knocked painfully against the wall, blood spilling from the wound. She crumpled to the ground with the animals still surrounding her. It hurt more than anything she had ever encountered and her vision was starting to get hazy. Blood was pouring from her head too quickly and with a soft whimper she looked around and saw Cia and Jash fall to the ground at the paws of the other animals. She wanted to wail with grief and terror but she couldn't make a sound as her vision went black and she fell unconscious.

After that, Saderia was just dimly aware of being dragged painfully up a flight of stairs. There was sticky stuff coating her fur and it made her very uncomfortable but she was barely aware of it. She had no concept of anything going on around her except for a few brief flashes of things. She was aware of being dragged to a different place and then to another place because beneath her it got slightly softer but sharper at some points. Unknown tortures poked at her, ripped her fur and she heard a faint rustling sound through the impenetrable darkness.

She was dragged somewhere else that she had no way of describing and finally she lay still, drifting off into blackness so complete it was terrifying. It could have been days or just a few hours that she lay there until she began to come around.

When she began to wake up, she started hearing murmuring voices that she couldn't completely make out. The murmuring grew clearer and she heard a few gasps and the sound of someone crying softly, though from sadness or joy, she wasn't sure. She was able to make out a female voice that sounded almost like her own--was she somehow talking? No, her mouth wasn't moving. And there was another male voice talking to the one that sounded like her.

Then there was the sound of somebody waking and then the sound of sheer panicking and claws scraping across a floor. The voices became very agitated, becoming louder and louder, faster and faster as the female voice and the male voice appeared to be trying to explain something to some very afraid animals. Finally the noise grew quieter and then there was a silence, as if whoever had woken up was taking in what the other voices said. Then there was a soft gasp, a rush of unidentifiable words and then there was another moment of panic, only this time when the voices settled down there was an undercurrent of worry and fear hanging in the air.

Saderia's amber eyes blinked open and she tried to look around but her sight was blurry and she didn't know where she was. As she became more focused, she realized that she had never been in this place before and couldn't recall how she had gotten there. Cold fear and panic swept over her with those realizations and she stumbled to her paws, trying to steady herself.

"Saderia!" The female voice sounded both overjoyed and worried at the same time.

Saderia turned toward the voice, her eyes widening as they came into focus and her sight lost the haze it had had before. In front of her stood two tigers, one a larger male with bright green eyes. But when Saderia looked at the other one, she felt as if she were looking directly into a mirror. The female tiger was smaller with the same glowing amber eyes, yellow orange fur and fluffy tail that Saderia had. There were bars separating her from them.

"Saderia!" the female exclaimed happily. Her voice sounded breathless, as if she couldn't believe what she was seeing. Tears teetered on her eyelids and she smiled a warm, caring smile. Her voice was both hopeful and horribly afraid, as if she were glad to see her, but at the same time deeply worried.

Saderia couldn't understand what was going on or where she was and she was feeling very panicked. And yet, this tiger's presence made her feel all right, maybe even better than she'd ever been in her life.

But there was something hauntingly familiar about the female tiger she was looking at and not just because she looked like an older copy of herself. Her heart started beating faster and she stared at the tiger in wonder, hope mixing with fear.

Her heartbeat sped up even more as the tiger beamed at her with warmth she had never experienced before. "Do you remember us?" the tiger asked.

Saderia shook her head numbly.

The tiger's smile grew a bit sad but still loving. "We've missed you so much!" she whispered, tears spilling over her cheeks. The male tiger nodded, his expression the same as the female tiger's.

"We thought we'd never see you again," he murmured.

There was something strangely familiar about him, too. Their voices made a memory stir inside her but she couldn't believe it. It was impossible...

Her amber eyes grew wider than ever before and her mouth dropped open as the female tiger whispered, "Saderia, I'm Karenisha, and this is Makero. We're your mother and father."

Chapter Nine

The Truth

"You can't be!" Saderia stammered. "Karenisha and Makero...my Mom and Dad...they're dead!"

The female tiger's amber eyes became pained and she looked down, blinking back tears. "We thought you were dead, too," she whispered.

Saderia shook her head back and forth in denial, tears trickling down her face. She wasn't aware of anything else around her and she stumbled backward a little. "You can't be!" she exclaimed. "You can't be! They're dead!"

It wasn't possible. It couldn't be true. Her parents had been pronounced dead ten years ago! Then she had another, scarier thought.

"Am I dead?" she whispered, panting in fear and confusion.

The female tiger looked up sharply but it was the male who answered.

"No, Saderia," he told her gently. "I know how confusing this must be. It's all going to be confusing for a while but you just have to trust us, all right? I'm your father..." His voice shook with emotion, and he blinked several times before going on. "And this is your mother."

The tiger, supposedly Karenisha, nodded. "We survived the fire. And we've missed you." She blinked rapidly, whispering, "It's been ten years, but you have to believe us. We survived, but we couldn't get back to you. Makero's right, and I know it's hard to believe, but it *is* us."

"But..." Saderia's sentence cut off and she crumpled on the ground sobbing.

Karenisha and Makero pressed to the bars of the cage they were in, their eyes wide with concern. "Saderia!" they both exclaimed.

"What's wrong?" Karenisha asked, her voice strained with worry.

Saderia just shook her head and pressed closer into a ball, trying to disappear. All her life she had wanted nothing more than to see her parents alive and there they were! They were perfect, just as she had thought they would be, and they looked exactly as she had remembered. They sounded and smelled and acted just like she recalled and how she had hoped they would. Karenisha was the exact image of her, just twenty-two years older-looking. But she knew that she wasn't what they had wanted. They had lived up to her expectations of perfection but she could not possibly live up to theirs.

But beside that, they weren't real; they couldn't be. So what was going on with her and why was she imagining things--just to hurt herself? Was this a dream? Was she still unconscious? But it didn't feel like a dream and she felt conscious. More than anything ever had, it felt *real*.

Karenisha and Makero were murmuring to each other and calling to her, their voices choked with worry and fear.

"Saderia! Please look up!" Karenisha called.

Very slowly, Saderia looked up at them. They were still there, which meant the dream still hadn't gone away...or it meant they were real.

"Can you please tell me what's wrong?" Karenisha asked gently. "We're here for you. Just tell us why you're crying."

"Because you're not real!" Saderia burst out, a new bout of tears making her voice quiver. "You can't possibly be real! I've spent ten years hoping you'd come back to me and I've dreamt of you being with me but it never happened and it never can! Karenisha and Makero died ten years ago in a fire!" She shook her head, trying to clear the tears as Karenisha and Makero went silent, staring at her in concern and sorrow.

"And you're perfect!" Saderia went on, still crying. "I'll never be good enough to deserve parents like you even if you aren't real! I've failed! I've ruined everything!"

"Don't talk like that!" Karenisha hissed. Softer, she went on, "You're more than we could have ever hoped for. Saderia, when I look at you now I see the exact image of myself, and that's amazing. Don't you realize that no matter what, you're still our daughter, and we care about you more than can ever be put into words? You've been more than 'good enough' since we first saw you. To us, you're perfect! Neither of us ever imagined a miracle like you could possibly be real, but now you are!"

Saderia closed her eyes and shook her head fiercely, sinking to her paws, shaking. Why couldn't she stop this painful dream?! Why was she hurting herself so much? What had she done to deserve this? Part of her wanted to pretend that they were real and go to enjoy being with them. But she knew that when she woke up there would be a huge hole in her and it would hurt her forever.

"Saderia!" Makero called. "Everything your mother said is true. You're an amazing girl and if you'd let us talk to you, you could tell us what we've missed in the past ten years." He took a deep, shaky breath. "We've missed ten years of your life. That's hurt us more than you can imagine and I'm sure it's hurt you, but please don't let us miss anymore of it."

Still shaking, Saderia shook her head, trying to shut the voices out of her mind. Maybe she was going insane after ten years of loneliness and pain and was imagining her parents because of that.

"How can we prove to you that we're real?" Karenisha pleaded.

"You can't! You're not!"

Karenisha's shaky breath was easily heard as she said, "Did you know I always wanted a daughter and I always wanted her to be named Saderia? That's you."

"I know that, I read it in your store room," she

whispered. "So it's just my imagination telling me that, since I know it."

"Do you know that I wrote that you were the best thing in my life when I had you? I said you would be smart and adventurous, kind but bold, and a truth-seeker. And I think you are all of those things, but you just can't see it."

"I already knew what you wrote. I found your diary and the key. Sorry for reading it, but that's just my imagination, too."

"You're stubborn like your mother," Makero said softly.

Very slowly Saderia looked up, not being able to count that as coming from her imagination.

She sniffed, tears still dripping down her face. "I am?"

They looked excited that they had gotten through to her. Makero nodded. "Definitely. Did you know that she will fight with anyone sometimes, just for the sake of arguing?"

Saderia shook her head.

Karenisha smiled and said, "Did you know your father tries to keep me from doing something crazy? That the reason we go well together is because we balance each other?"

Again, she shook her head.

Karenisha beckoned for her to come over to them with her fluffy tail. "It doesn't always hurt to let someone in," she told her gently. "When you open yourself to love someone, they can always hurt you, but they can also help you. Like everything in life, loving somebody is taking a risk, but sometimes it's definitely worth it."

Her words were kind and wise and Saderia found herself hesitantly stepping over to them.

"We've always taken that risk," Makero murmured with a slight smile as she stepped up to the bars separating them. She didn't wonder about the bars yet, though they certainly didn't make any sense.

Instead she hesitantly put her paw up to the bars. Karenisha and Makero touched their paws to hers through the bars and Saderia felt a warm glow spread through her. It felt more real than anything she had ever experienced and, very slowly, she pressed closer to the bars. They did the same. She paused for a very long moment before slowly lifting her head to look her father in the eyes. His eyes smiled back at her, and for a moment Saderia felt warm and safe in their green depths before she turned away to stare into her mother's amber eyes. In it she saw all the love and affection she had wished for every night of her life.

She looked at both of them. "Mom?" she whispered. "Dad?"

Both of them broke out in huge smiles and pressed even closer against the bars. Saderia did the same and closed her eyes for a moment, hoping with all her heart that this was real and she wasn't just setting herself up for more pain. But she realized that she didn't care anymore. She longed to stay there forever. But now new questions buzzed around in her mind.

She pulled away from the bars a bit and faced Karenisha and Makero's shining faces.

"Oh, Saderia, we've missed you for so long!" Karenisha exclaimed.

"We always hoped you were alive and we never stopped thinking about you, and hoping you were safe," Makero told her. "We never stopped worrying about you."

"We tried to get to you," Karenisha went on. "I would have fought forever if it meant I could see you, but I couldn't! I'm so sorry, Saderia. I know how much pain all of this has brought."

"It has," Saderia whispered, her voice quavering with emotion. "What happened? Why did you just disappear ten years ago?"

Their faces grew instantly dark and they both looked down. There was a long moment of silence and Saderia began to feel alarmed. Had she ruined this moment and turned her parents against her when she had just found them? The fear made her want to start crying again but then Karenisha spoke.

"Saderia, I know this is hard, but it's about to get even harder. But it can't be avoided." Taking a deep, long breath, she sighed, "Look around you. We won't go anywhere, I promise."

Saderia stared at them a moment longer, unsure of whether to believe that or not. But she finally decided that her parents wouldn't lie to her and bravely turned around to take in her surroundings. Her eyes widened in confusion as she took everything in, wondering with new fear what could possibly be going on.

Long, cage bars surrounded her in one cell, and her parents in another. She could see the bars form another cage behind her parents but she couldn't see inside it from where she was. But why was she in a cage? She looked around at her own cage and noticed a curious metal slate screwed into the wall over the part of her cage where the bars met the wall. The rest of the place she was in was dank and dark; she was barely able to see through the darkness. There was a little rocky path leading to all three cages and then there was a dirty stairway leading to somewhere she didn't know.

Her heart began to beat wildly as she realized she was in a dungeon. Turning to her parents, she briefly felt a stab of relief that they had kept their promise and were still there. But before she could ask them where they were, a voice came from the third cage.

"Saderia? Is that you?" The voice was worried and very familiar; Saderia felt a trickle of fear and uncertainty.

Karenisha and Makero moved slightly to the side so that Saderia could look across their cage into the next one. She gasped when she made out the shapes of Cia and Uncle Jash! What were they doing there? How'd she get there anyway?

Her aunt and uncle's blue eyes widened with recognition when they saw her and let out a gasp at the same time she did.

"Cia?!" she gasped. "Uncle Jash?!"

"Saderia?!" they both exclaimed at the same time.

The two of them looked terrified and confused and they avoided looking at Karenisha and Makero as if, like her, they couldn't believe they were real.

"What are you doing here?" she called.

"What is this place?" Cia asked at the same time.

All three of them turned to Karenisha and Makero for an explanation. Saderia felt a rush of happiness when she looked at her parents again but she saw the color drain from her aunt and uncle's faces when they looked their way.

"K-Karenisha?" Cia stammered.

"Now, Cia, we've been through this," Karenisha said patiently. "I am alive, and Makero is alive. There's nothing to be afraid of, okay?"

Cia nodded meekly but Uncle Jash still looked spooked.

"So you didn't kill them?" Saderia blurted, her head hurting. If Karenisha and Makero weren't dead, then no one had killed them and maybe no one had caused the fire, but if they hadn't been dead, then where had they been for ten years? And if they had been here, then where was 'here,' why *were* they there, why had they been there for ten years and why had she never known the truth about any of it?

Cia, Uncle Jash, Karenisha and Makero all turned to her in shock at the question.

"Of course not!" Cia exclaimed, her eyes wide with shock. "Karenisha is my sister! I would never do anything like that!"

Uncle Jash nodded meekly. "How could you think that?"

Karenisha and Makero turned to her with confused expressions.

"I'm sorry," Saderia stammered. "I just found so much evidence and it…it seemed kind of likely."

"Evidence?" Uncle Jash asked.

"I…I found cans of gasoline hidden outside the house and…"

"He must have put them there," Karenisha hissed bitterly, interrupting her.

Cia, Uncle Jash and Saderia turned to Karenisha and Makero.

"'He?'" Saderia asked, "Who's 'he?'"

The two tigers slowly looked around at everyone and let out a long, collective sigh.

"Maybe it's about time everyone knew what was going on," Karenisha murmured.

Saderia felt the fur along her back begin to stand up. She knew she was on the verge of learning some new, amazing secret, one that might explain everything she had wondered about. For a moment she was afraid to hear it but a rush of determination to know the truth filled her from head to tail-tip and she sat up straighter.

"I'm ready," she announced. "I can take it. I need the truth."

Karenisha's head whipped around to stare at her daughter in equal amounts of wonder and admiration. There was an undercurrent of concern for Saderia, though she smiled weakly at her. But her smile turned down quickly and she took a deep breath before asking, "Cia? Jash? Are you ready, as well?"

They both exchanged a terrified glance before nodding meekly.

Karenisha took another deep breath and then let it out. "All right. You all know of the fire ten years ago," she began. "Well, it was all planned. Gasoline was spread and it was meant to separate us from everyone else so that we couldn't get any help. That's how we were captured and we've been prisoners for ten years. We've tried to escape, but have always failed." Letting out a sad sigh she continued, "Anyway, the gasoline cans Saderia mentioned must have been hidden there because he might have wanted to frame Cia and Jash at some point."

"Who's 'he?'" Saderia repeated.

Karenisha opened her mouth to reply, but at that moment a door let out a long creak and every head whipped around to stare at the huge staircase. As she stared, Saderia was able to make out amber eyes gleaming with triumph in the blackness and then she was able to see the dark brown fur and pitch black mane. She gasped and took a step back in her cage.

"What are you doing here?" she exclaimed.

Cia and Uncle Jash both gasped and backed away while Karenisha and Makero sprung to the front of their cage, hissing and snarling.

Dastarius descended the rest of the stairs, sneering at all of them condescendingly.

"I think it's about time you figured it out, Princess," Dastarius snarled cruelly as he passed her locked cage, still smirking.

Horror made her stop breathing for a moment as she began to put things together. Her head whipped around to stare at her parents as he approached their cage.

Over in their own cage, Cia and Uncle Jash had gone pale.

"Dastarius?" Cia exclaimed. "How...What are you doing here?! What did you...?" She trailed off and Dastarius ignored her, focusing on Karenisha instead.

"Well, Karenisha? I've got your daughter now," he snarled. "Are you going to finally give me what I want?"

Karenisha glared at him, hissing, but her amber gaze became uncertain and she took a step back. Makero jumped in front of her and snarled at Dastarius. "Stay away from her," he roared. "Don't you dare hurt Saderia!"

Dastarius's eyes gleamed. "Then tell the ex-

Queen to tell me what I need to know."

"Never!" Karenisha hissed, taking a step forward to stand beside Makero. "It's for the royal family only, and you're not part of that!" She narrowed her eyes. "And if you make one move toward Saderia, I will rip you to shreds."

"That's going to be rather difficult, Karenisha, considering you're in a cage."

Makero narrowed his eyes and let out an outraged roar while Karenisha scraped the bars of the cage with her claws, trying to scratch him.

"If you tell me, I'll let her live," he promised with a cold sneer.

Karenisha and Makero were shaking with rage but a flash of helplessness crossed their faces.

Dastarius saw it and his grin grew wider. "I'm sure you'll tell me after watching her suffer for a while," he hissed quietly, before turning around to stalk away back up the stairs, casting one last evil, triumphant glance at Saderia before he closed the door behind him, leaving them alone.

A long moment of utter silence settled over them and everyone sat absolutely still, trying to comprehend what had happened. Finally Saderia couldn't take it and she turned to her parents with a pleading expression.

"What is going on?" she whispered.

They exchanged a glance and then stepped closer to her, still looking shaken and horrified. Saderia could still see Cia and Uncle Jash who exchanged a quick glance before stepping closer to the bars of their cage to hear what Karenisha and Makero were going to say.

"Dastarius is the one that started the fire," Karenisha whispered bitterly. "He's the one that captured us, and kept us away from you, Saderia. He's been plotting to take over the throne for a long time, and now..." She shook her head, unable to continue.

Cia and Uncle Jash were appalled. "But...he..." Cia trailed off, looking horrified and scared. "What...?"

Saderia couldn't say anything but she didn't need to because Karenisha went on, "He was probably planning to frame you if anyone got suspicious, Cia, Jash. Or make everyone forget about us, whichever worked better."

"So...Dastarius...he did all this?" Saderia whispered finally. "When you trusted him so much and Cia and Uncle Jash trusted him and...he set up all the websites...and what about the books in the library? He started the fire, then tried to frame Cia and Uncle Jash... And I believed him for a while..."

Karenisha stiffened. "You knew him?"

Saderia nodded numbly. "I met him at a royal meeting place and I had this bad feeling about him. I...I didn't understand it before but now..." Tears pricked her eyes. "I've been so stupid! I should have trusted that feeling! I should have *done* something! Now it's too late!"

"Saderia, calm down," Makero said gently. "It's all right. You had no way of knowing. Go on with your story. What do you mean by all that? What's happened?"

Cia and Uncle Jash looked equally confused and turned to Saderia for answers.

Saderia took a deep breath, on the verge of tears, knowing she'd have to tell them everything before she got any answers of her own. So she started at the beginning and told them about the first dream she had about the fire. She talked about the scene she had witnessed when she went to her parent's room and how she had gotten the diary. She told about how she had met Dastarius and how he had stuck up for her, probably just to gain her trust to frame Cia and Uncle Jash or capture her, she now realized. How she had searched for her mother's diary key and found the compartment in Cia's closet, then the locked door in the library that hid the good biographies.

"Dastarius must have hidden them in there," Karenisha interrupted angrily. "He must have been trying to make the other animals forget about us so he could take over and there would be no question about it."

"But if Dastarius locked the books in there, then how did Cia have the key on that ring?" Saderia asked confused.

"I just found it one day," Cia told her, looking just as confused. "I found it after Karenisha di-- well, after she disappeared. It was on one of the shelves in the library. The librarians didn't know where it went so I just kept it. I never knew where it went either."

"Dastarius must have left it there on accident," Karenisha muttered. "Cia finding it must have been good luck for him to try to frame her."

Saderia nodded slowly, trying to absorb it all. She continued on with her story of all that had happened, about finding the door in her mother's closet and then the key to her diary and reading all the entries. She told them how she had used Cia's ring of keys to open the door to Karenisha's store room and then the dungeon and how she had put her name on the scroll.

"What I don't understand is why you just now went into those rooms," Karenisha said, adding more gently, "Were you too scared before?"

"Actually, I just found out about them recently."

Her eyes widened and she turned to Cia. "You never told her about the secret rooms?!"

"Why should I?" Cia retorted. "She didn't need to know about them!"

"Yes she did! She would have found them later on, like she did, and been confused, like she was! Wouldn't it have been better if you told her?!"

"Why *didn't* you tell me?" Saderia asked cautiously.

Cia hesitated. "I didn't tell you about the secret rooms because one of them was your mother's store room and I didn't want you to get upset about seeing your mother's things when we thought she was dead." Her voice quavered. "I just tried to do what was best for you."

"I guess that sort of makes sense," Karenisha conceded a bit softly.

"Why didn't you just ask me what *I* thought was best for me?" Saderia asked quietly.

Cia opened her mouth to answer but then closed it, eyes widening as she turned away.

A frown creased Karenisha's face. "What do you mean by that?" she asked her daughter.

"Well, Cia and Uncle Jash have always done what *they* thought would be best for me," Saderia explained. "I don't go to school like I want to; I have tutors. I don't have any friends; I just go to the royal meetings and mingle with the advisors there. I don't get to go outside as often as I want to; I get to stay inside and not get dirty like a good Princess. I don't get to look how I want to; Cia and Uncle Jash always make me wear accessories and stuff to look like a typical Princess and I always have to fake being happy because then others get mad because they think I have a perfect life. I don't get to have any fun like play and stuff; like I said, I have to act like a typical Princess all the time."

There was a long beat of silence and then Karenisha turned to Cia with blazing eyes. "And to think I trusted you to raise my daughter when I was gone!" she shouted. "Ha! All you've done is made the first ten years of her life miserable!"

"I..."

"Did you ever think that maybe she'd want something different?" Karenisha interrupted Cia. "Did you ever think that maybe she had her own mind and her own ideas?! She's just a kid! Did you ever ask her what she'd want?"

"Well, no, but I didn't think..."

"No, you didn't! Not in the least bit did you think! Children aren't just something you can control, Cia! They have feelings, too, and they see things differently! They don't just do what you tell them and they shouldn't have to live without their own say!" She glared at her sister. "I can't believe you'd be so self-centered, so selfish, so stupid, so..."

"Karenisha," Makero interrupted her softly. "Calm down for a minute. Cia was probably just trying to do what she thought was best, all right? She doesn't really understand any of that; she's not a parent. Anyway, there's nothing that can be done about it now, so just let it go."

Karenisha hissed and pointedly turned her back on Cia, but said nothing more. Terrible pain flashed in Cia's eyes that Karenisha was so angry with her when they had just been reunited after ten long, grief-filled years. Guilt and horror made her aunt look sickly pale. Saderia could tell she was blinking back tears and quickly stepped up to press against her parent's cage, looking at her aunt and uncle.

"Cia, it's all right," she told her aunt gently. "I

know you were just trying to help raise me. I'm not mad at you or anything. Like Dad said, there's nothing that can be done now. Sometimes we make mistakes, but it's all right. Mistakes are made to learn from them, aren't they? Not to make us miserable."

Cia blinked at Saderia, tears teetering on her eyelids. "Are...are you sure?" Her voice sounded choked. "Because I never meant to..."

"I'm sure," Saderia said. "I understand. And I do appreciate you taking care of me because I wasn't exactly the best tiger to take care of either. I'll forgive you if you forgive me."

Cia bit her lip to keep it from trembling and nodded briskly. "Okay," she managed. "I'm sorry."

Saderia smiled weakly at her and nodded. "I'm sorry, too."

"Karenisha," Makero murmured to her quietly, angling his ears in Cia's direction.

Karenisha looked at him with narrowed eyes then let out a long sigh, tears in her eyes. She turned to Cia. "I'm sorry, too," she told her gently. "I know you didn't mean any harm. I don't hate you or anything. I'm still glad that I finally got to see you and Jash." She shook her head with a painful sigh. "I really am sorry for yelling. I'm just...upset..." She blinked tears away. "Just upset that I missed ten years of my daughter's life."

Cia nodded more slowly, with a weak smile. "It's okay, Karenisha. I...I understand. I'm sorry, though, because you're right. I...I shouldn't have been so ignorant and cold."

Karenisha looked down. "It's good to see you. You too, Jash."

Uncle Jash just nodded, still looking shocked. Saderia could sympathize with him. What had already happened was a lot for anybody to take in.

"It's…good to see you, too, Karenisha…Makero…" Uncle Jash stammered. He turned to Saderia. "Um…continue with your story."

"Yes, continue," Makero echoed. "What else happened?"

Saderia resumed telling them about how she had gone to the library and found the websites that said horrible things about her parents, all of it so obviously untrue now, and how she had first started to suspect that something was wrong because it said the fire had been planned. She told them about how Dastarius had talked to her and given her the impression that Cia and Uncle Jash did it. Karenisha and Makero tensed when they heard that their daughter had been around him but nodded stiffly for her to go on. She told them about finding the room in the library and how she started suspecting Cia and Uncle Jash, then. Then she talked about how she had found the gasoline and going to Dastarius's house to talk to him and about hearing Cia say…

"If you didn't do anything, then what was that about?" Saderia asked Cia. "I heard you say to Uncle Jash that I 'cannot be Queen now or ever!' and that you'll 'make sure of that.' It sounded almost like you were, well...planning to get rid of me."

"What?" Uncle Jash exclaimed. "No, that's definitely not it!"

"We would never do anything like that!" Cia echoed.

Uncle Jash calmed down slightly. "Cia was just worried about you. She noticed how upset you were and was talking about how you had never gotten over your parents, um...death." He shot a glance at Karenisha and Makero who gave him a tight smile to show that it was okay. Uncle Jash went on, "She was saying how you couldn't be Queen if you were to keep on that way."

"Yes, I was kind of upset about it," Cia admitted. "It hurt me, too, the way you were so upset about Karenisha and Makero's...passing because then I thought about it, too. I wanted you to get over it so I could get past it myself."

"Right," Uncle Jash agreed. "And when she said 'I'll make sure of that,' she meant that she'd do something to try to make you get over Karenisha and Makero's deaths. I had asked her if she were really going to do whatever it took to make you forget about it."

"I guess that was a mean thing, too," Cia admitted. "But not as bad as what you thought."

Saderia thought it over carefully. "It makes sense now..." she murmured. "I'm really sorry for suspecting you guys. It...it must have really hurt you when I accused you..."

"It's all right," Cia said gently. "We can understand now."

Uncle Jash managed a tight smile. "Go on."

Saderia told them how she had accused Cia and Uncle Jash then run away from the house, spending the night in the woods. She told them how all the animals had acted like they were annoyed with her because they thought she was just some spoiled Princess.

"We're really sorry about that," Cia apologized. "We didn't think about that. We were just worried about you and were looking for you."

Saderia forgave them and went on with her story, about how she had met up with Dastarius and gone to his house. She realized that must be where she was now and with a sharp pang of horror and despair, she realized how close she had been to her parents without ever knowing it. The room above them that led down to the dungeon must have been behind that locked door in the hall. All along, she could have done something but hadn't.

"You didn't know," Karenisha murmured stiffly, guessing what she was thinking. She and Makero had tensed when she told them about how she had gone to Dastarius's house and she could easily understand that.

"I just feel so stupid," Saderia muttered.

"You didn't know," Makero repeated. "Don't beat yourself up about it. There was nothing you could have done anyway. We'd still be locked up."

Suppressing a shiver, Saderia finished by telling the last part of how she'd gone home for her mother's diary but Cia and Uncle Jash had run in and they'd hidden from the animals.

"Who were they anyway?" Saderia asked Cia and Uncle Jash, shivering as she remembered.

"Do you remember how we were telling you about the animals whose children were kidnapped?" Cia asked. "Well, that was them. All the bad things that happened to them must have made them desperate."

"Dastarius must have turned them against you," Makero agreed gravely. "He must have convinced them that you were doing nothing and that he could help them if they did whatever he wanted." He hissed in disgust.

"Wow," Saderia muttered. There was so much to take in and she still had more questions. She turned to Karenisha and Makero. "Could Dastarius actually take over?"

"He might," Makero answered her. "The five of us are the last of the royal family. He got us first and then if he got you, all of the royal family would be gone and there would be no one to rule the forest. Well, that creates the problem of who *is* going to rule the forest. Since he was such a trusted and powerful advisor," he spat the words angrily, "he might be able to take over after coming up with a good excuse."

"Especially if he had the Power," Karenisha murmured.

"The 'Power?'" Saderia asked. "What do you mean by that?"

Karenisha looked uncertain. Makero touched her shoulder with the tip of his tail gently. "It's okay, you can tell them. Dastarius won't get any new information out of it and I don't think just the first part will endanger them."

Karenisha hesitated for a moment longer but finally nodded, accepting it. "Okay. Saderia, you said you read my diary, right? Well, on one of the pages it says that my mother told me about a power that had been passed down through the generations of the royal family. Some animals got it stronger than others and some weaker than others but it was always passed down. This power that was passed on was...well, it was sort of like being psychic. Some members of the royal family have the power to see the future in dreams. For some it's clearer than others."

Saderia blinked in shock. See the future? In dreams? Suddenly she thought back to all the dreams she'd had and with a jolt she realized that some of them had hinted at what had happened. In a way, the dreams had led her to do all of the things she did, so was it possible that she had this strange new power?

She looked to see how Cia and Uncle Jash would react. Uncle Jash was shocked but Cia just sat there calmly.

"Cia knows a little about it," Karenisha said. "I

have the Power and I have dreams about the future sometimes, but she doesn't. She used to help me try to figure them out but my future sight isn't as clear as some before me and so I don't like to jump to any conclusions."

"I never...you never told me..." Uncle Jash gasped, looking at Cia and Karenisha. "Is that even possible?"

Karenisha smiled weakly. "Yes, it's possible. It's happened to me before. And we're very sorry for not telling you, Jash, but it's best that as few animals as possible know. It's a big and powerful secret; only one royal animal per generation gets it. And the first few generations of our family had to read a scroll to get the power, but then it was passed down. That scroll is hidden in our oldest ancestor, Queen Tarae's, tomb but it is locked with a code. Reading the scroll aloud can give any animal the Power and it is very special and powerful." She sighed. "Dastarius knows all that and he wants the Power badly. He knows that if he had the Power, the forest would accept him as the new King of the forest more easily, less questions asked. That's how important it is." Going on, she said, "Only I know where Queen Tarae's tomb is and what the code is to unlock it. But Dastarius knows that I know. That's why he's kept us alive for ten years; he tried to force me to tell him where and how to get the scroll but I've refused."

"That's what he was doing when he came down here a few minutes ago," Makero added. "He thinks we both know, though, which is why he kept me alive for so long, too."

Saderia shivered at the thought that her parents had just barely escaped being slaughtered, and only because they knew something that could help that monster control the whole forest! Then she had a worse, darker thought. "And now that he's got me, he's planning to threaten me to get you to talk," she whispered softly.

Karenisha froze and Saderia saw a look of intense pain flash in her amber eyes. She squeezed her eyes shut tightly, taking a deep breath. Makero wrapped his tail around her gently and she finally opened her eyes, now bright with pain. "Yes," she whispered.

Saderia was silent for a long moment and then finally murmured, "Don't do it, Mom. Whatever he does to me, don't do it. You have to watch out for the forest and we can't let him win and take over. Whatever happens, don't tell him."

Karenisha's eyes glittered with pain and admiration. "That's brave of you, Saderia, but I don't think I'm as strong as you. I think he might win."

"No!" Saderia shouted. "He can't win! Not after what he's done! You can't tell him! You can't let him win!"

"Saderia, it's been hard, but if he does something to you…" Her voice caught and Makero took up for her.

"We've spent ten years hoping you were alive

and worrying about if you were okay. Now we finally get to see you and it is under such horrid circumstances. We can't just loose you so soon afterward…"

Karenisha nodded sadly but then a fierce fury lit up her eyes. "If he lays a paw on her, I'll kill him," she hissed. "I don't know how, but I'll find a way to get revenge!"

Silence fell and lasted before Saderia felt the need to speak up and change the subject. "Do you think I might have that Power?"

"Have you had any dreams?" Karenisha asked her, starting to calm down. "Not just normal ones, but ones that feel real, ones that feel like they're trying to tell you something."

Thinking back to the strange dreams she had had in the past few weeks, she realized that was exactly what it felt like and nodded meekly. "Yes, I have. So I…"

Karenisha smiled a weak smile. "You have it," she announced.

"Isn't there something about the fiftieth generation or something?" Makero asked Karenisha. "Didn't you say something about that one time?"

Karenisha's face darkened. "No," she said too quickly. "I don't know anything about that."

"Karenisha," Makero murmured. "Don't you think they should know everything?"

"I'm not giving that psycho any other reason to keep Saderia," she spat. "Besides, I don't even know what it's supposed to be, just some weird, old prophetic thing. Nobody knows what it's really about. It's in the scroll."

Saderia and Makero both decided to let it drop and there was a long, horrible moment of silence. Saderia didn't want to have to realize it, but she was beginning to be aware of something horrible. Karenisha and Makero had been trapped for ten years...

"We're never getting out of here, are we?"

Cia and Uncle Jash turned to Karenisha and Makero with terrified expressions, while Karenisha and Makero stiffened and looked down. Nobody answered, and that was an answer in itself.

Chapter Ten

Way to Freedom

The first night Saderia was in the dungeon, she didn't want to sleep although her body was begging for rest. She hadn't had anything to eat all day and it would be nice to escape the emptiness of her belly with rest, but she forced her eyes to stay open. She was afraid that if she slept, Karenisha and Makero would be gone in the morning and she would realize that nothing had been real after all. But Karenisha and Makero were endlessly coaxing her to sleep and they finally convinced her by telling her to sleep close to their cage.

With their fur brushing through the bars, Saderia finally allowed herself to rest, telling herself that she would wake up if she felt the warmth of their presence disappearing or their slow breathing fading away. She drifted into a deep sleep which no dreams disturbed and when she thought about it later, it bothered her. If she was supposed to have a strange power, then why wasn't it working when she needed it the most?

In the morning she was relieved to see that her parents had kept their promise to stay where they were and was delighted that they were real, after all. But with the happiness came fear because if everything were real, that meant her being trapped was real, too. Occasionally she tortured herself by wondering whether she'd rather be at home, safe, instead of trapped and starving, but with her parents. She convinced herself that she would always prefer the last one, and in her heart she knew it was true.

Several days passed; she had no way of knowing how many. Every day was the same as the next, wake up in the cell, talk to her parents about her life that they had missed, be happy, be scared, fall asleep, wake up. By now, she was starving because they hadn't been fed at all in the past few days. Her parents told her that they had been fed before but now he was just torturing them.

Surprisingly, though it hurt, Saderia didn't mind because it felt better in there than in any other place. It was a strange thing to be happy in a dungeon but she was and knowing that lifted her spirits. It was because she had finally gotten the truth instead of a mix of lies, and because she had finally found her parents that she had wished for all her life. She got scared and upset, of course, but with Karenisha and Makero there, she was able to get through it. And she always tried to hide how upset and scared she was because it would hurt her parents.

Cia and Uncle Jash, opposite her, were terrified. She could tell they felt bad about it because, like her, they were relieved at finding Karenisha and Makero alive and felt they should show it. Saderia and her parents understood them, though, and weren't mad at them in the least bit. They were in a state of shock at first and rarely talked, but after a while they must have decided to make the most of it and talked to everyone again.

Silence wasn't a bad thing, except that when there was silence, they were forced to think about their situation. They all grew used to it, though, and sometimes it was good to be able to think without having to worry about the others being mad at them. It was just so natural when there were no words to fill the time. Saderia often berated herself for not being able to figure everything out but she finally accepted that she had had no way of knowing and couldn't have done anything.

She hated Dastarius for tricking her and doing this to her. Often she wondered what he was doing, if he was setting something up to fake their death or if anyone knew they were missing yet. Maybe he was waiting for Karenisha to tell him how to get into that tomb. Hopefully he would be waiting a long time then. Saderia hadn't tried to get her mother to tell her the code because the less she knew, the better it was. If she knew, Dastarius would just torment her to get it out of her. Worse, he would torment the ones she cared about to get her to talk.

On one day, something unusual did happen, though. The door at the top of the staircase opened, and Dastarius stepped down the stairs, wearing his cocky sneer. Karenisha and Makero immediately jumped to their paws to hiss and snarl at him and demand freedom. Cia and Uncle Jash just stumbled to the back of their cages, in shock all over again. But Saderia was right at the front of her cage, separated from her parents only by bars, snarling at Dastarius with all the hatred she had ever felt.

"You tricked me!" she snarled. "As soon as I'm out of here, I'll get my revenge! You'll never win!"

"You won't get out of there," Dastarius replied calmly. "And I can't see you getting revenge considering how weak and hungry you are." He cast a vindictive glance at Karenisha and Makero who just narrowed their eyes and increased the volume of their snarls.

Saderia glared at him. "What do you want?"

"I think you know what I want." He said it to Karenisha.

Karenisha hissed at him. "Forget it! I'll never tell you!"

"Then maybe you'll tell your daughter," he growled, with a curious look at Saderia. "Maybe she already knows."

"She knows nothing! Only I know the code so leave her alone!" Karenisha snarled.

"Only you know the code. Then I guess I'll just have to find some way to make you tell me."

"There's no way!"

Dastarius raised an eyebrow. "Do you remember what it's like to be fed? I think your daughter does. I'm sure it's hard on her to go from pampered

Princess to dirty, starving captive. If you don't want your daughter to die from painful starvation, I suggest you tell me."

Karenisha narrowed her eyes and backed away, looking suddenly scared. She said nothing.

"Do you really want to your daughter to die?" Dastarius went on coldly. "Would you rather watch her die, or tell me what I need to know? Your choice, Karenisha."

Karenisha started shaking, looking horrified and afraid now. She cast a painful glance at Saderia's gaunt appearance and sorrow flashed in her eyes. Her gaze returned to Dastarius, scared and pleading.

"Your choice," he repeated.

Saderia couldn't let it happen. "Don't tell him!" she shouted. "I'm fine, Mom! I'm going to be okay! Don't tell him!"

Dastarius glared at her. "Stay out of this!" He swiped a claw through the bars and a gash sliced across her forehead. Blood began dripping out of the wound as Saderia took several steps back from the bars, struggling not to wince or show any sign of pain for her mother's sake, even though it did hurt.

Karenisha and Makero pressed up against the bars that separated them, their faces alarmed. Cia and Uncle Jash let out gasps and pressed against the bars of their cages, too, looking terrified.

"Guys, it's okay," Saderia said carefully. "I'm all right." Glaring at Dastarius, she added, "It didn't hurt at all."

Dastarius ignored her except for a growl and kept his gaze trained on Karenisha. "You'll tell me after she's suffered a while longer. And if I have to wait till she's dead, I will."

Makero snarled fiercely at him. "Leave my daughter alone!"

Dastarius just sneered at him before turning around to leave. As soon as the door atop the stairs shut behind him, Karenisha demanded, "Are you okay? Does it hurt?"

"No, Mom. I'm okay, really. You don't have to worry about me. I'm far from a pampered Princess; I can take it."

They both hesitated then Karenisha murmured, "If you're sure…"

"I am."

Makero growled to himself. "You shouldn't have to take this."

"Neither should you," she pointed out. "Don't let him get to you."

"That's kind of hard," Cia commented.

"How can he not get to us? We're in a dunge-on!" Uncle Jash agreed.

Saderia sighed and decided to get off that morbid topic, saying the first thing that came to mind. "So what does Dastarius do while we're down here? Apart from plotting how to take over the forest, I mean."

"Put on an act for everyone else," Karenisha

muttered.

"And fight with his son," Makero added disgustedly.

Saderia frowned. "Dastarius has a son?"

Cia and Uncle Jash looked surprised, too, but Karenisha and Makero nodded simultaneously.

"What's he like?" Saderia asked curiously.

"Who knows?" Makero muttered. "Probably as bad as his father. How else would he be?"

"Probably," Karenisha agreed.

"What's his name?"

"I can't think of it now, but I'll know it when I hear it," Karenisha told her.

Saderia was silent for a moment. Why had she never heard of him or seen him at Dastarius's house? But she just let it drop, having no answers to those questions, trying to ignore the curiosity it inspired. She sighed. "You guys survived ten years in here?"

"There was a lot of moving around at first," Karenisha told her. "We tried to escape a few times but never succeeded."

"Oh."

After a while, Saderia curled up to sleep, having nothing better to do. Her body told her she needed to rest and so she obeyed, not caring what time it was outside the horrible dungeon. But that night wasn't like the other nights, the difference being that a dream was unfolding in her mind.

In the dream, Saderia could hear the swish of keys and she felt cramped, as if she were in a small space. Then all of a sudden a flash of light lit up the dream, strange because she hadn't seen real light since she had awoke in the dungeon. Lit up by the beautiful, natural light was a strange shack out in the middle of some woods, but the moment she saw it, it disappeared to be replaced by darkness followed by words. The words were almost inaudible but by straining herself to hear in her dream, she was able to make out, "He'll kill me if he finds out, but I want to help you…"

Saderia awoke with a gasp, probably in the middle of the night and looked around fearfully, wondering what her dream could mean. She felt a stir of hope inside her when she remembered that her dream said someone would help someone. Did that mean someone would help her escape? She wanted to wake up her mother and tell her about the dream so that they might be able to figure it out together but at that moment, she realized something was different.

The changes were hardly noticeable; it was slightly lighter inside the dungeon, a bit of fresher air drifted in from the top of the staircase, and another's quicker breathing joined the deep, sleep breathing of her family. Saderia felt fear shoot up her spine as she turned to the door at the top of the staircase. She couldn't see anything but she knew someone was there. Not knowing what to do, she stayed silent and the silence lasted for a very long time. Saderia had just begun to think she had imagined the changes when a timid voice whispered, "Is anyone awake?"

Saderia stayed absolutely still, not knowing if she should answer or not. By the quick breathing, she could tell that whoever had spoken was feeling panicked. Eventually she whispered back, "Who's asking?"

There was a quick scraping sound as if whoever was there had jumped at the sound of her voice, and the breathing quickened until whoever it was got themselves together. "I can't tell you," the voice replied. "Who are you?"

"I can't tell *you*," she retorted.

"I can just come down and find out," it threatened.

"What's stopping you?" Saderia growled back coolly.

There was a pause. "Well, then you'll see me too. I don't even want to be here."

"So why are you?" She could tell by now that the voice didn't belong to her jailor, Dastarius. It was a male voice, but a bit softer and slightly nicer, and obviously scared. Wondering who it could possibly be, she squinted to try to make out the shape at the top of the steps, but she couldn't. "Look, what do you want?"

"Well...you're, uh, *innocent*, right?" he asked cautiously.

"Um...I guess."

"I mean, Dastarius captured you because he wants the throne, because he's a power-hungry psycho, not because you did anything wrong, right?"

"Right," Saderia said suspiciously. She was already curious about who it was but now she was suspicious when he lingered on the *Da* part of Dastarius's name, quickly slurring it into the last part to make it right. "What are you doing here?"

He paused for a long moment, then whispered even more softly than before, "He'll kill me if he finds out, but I want to help you."

Saderia's eyes widened and she took a few paces back, her claws scrabbling on the stone underneath her. Whoever it was had just repeated the exact same message from her dream! Suddenly she realized what he was saying and she let out a soft gasp. "You can...help?" she whispered. "You mean, you can help me escape this place?"

Again, he hesitated. "Yes," he muttered softly. For some reason, he didn't sound too happy about that. He sounded frightened and unsure, but Saderia could tell he meant what he said, even if she didn't know who it was.

"How?" she hissed. "And who are you?"

"I can't tell you!" he hissed back, a bit angrily, but with fear making his voice higher. "He'll kill me if he knows!"

"Dastarius? Okay, okay, sorry. It's just kind of hard to trust somebody when you can't even see them."

"You don't exactly have a great choice," he replied. "You can either trust me to get you out or stay down there."

"I'll take the first option."

"All right. If it helps, I...I hate Dastarius as much as you do." Saderia grew even more suspicious when she heard the regretful tone in his voice and how he once again lingered on the first syllable of the evil lion's name. But, as he had said, she really had no choice.

"Okay," she said slowly. "How can you help me get out?"

Whoever was talking took a deep breath and said a little shakily, "I'm sorry but I don't know where the keys are or I'd unlock the cages. But there's another way out. Do you know about the slate screwed into the wall in one of the cages?"

"Yes, it's in my cage. What does it have to do with escaping?"

"Well, behind it is an air vent, an escape route."

Saderia's ears pricked up and excitement filled her. A real escape route! But then suspicion clouded her mind as she thought it through. "Why would a dungeon need air conditioning?" she snapped. "Is this some sort of trap?"

"No!" he exclaimed quickly. Only slightly calmer, he explained, "This wasn't always a dungeon. It used to just be a cellar and that's why there's an air vent. Dastarius turned it into a dungeon when he went after the throne and he put that slate over the vent so no one could escape."

"So this is really an escape route?"

"Yes, you have to believe me. If you don't, he'll kill you!"

Saderia thought about it and decided that he was right and she did have to believe that, and she found that she did. "Okay, I guess I believe you. But where does this vent lead?"

"To the kitchen in Dastarius's house. There's a door that leads to the screen porch which leads outside, so you can escape that way."

Excitement skated through her as she thought about the prospect of freedom, but suddenly she realized that it was too easy and said, "Okay, that's great, but it's screwed into the wall. How am I supposed to get in it?"

There was a moment of silence and then Saderia jumped as something hit the stone floor with a loud crack. Padding forward she saw a screwdriver lying just outside of her cage. She swiped her paw through the bars and tugged the screwdriver toward her, then looked back toward the stairs when whoever it was started speaking again.

"Just unscrew the slate and there will be a grate over the vent, but you'll be able to get that off. Then just follow the vent up and then straight. At the very end it'll turn to the right and into the vent that's in the kitchen. I already unscrewed that one so you'll be able to get past it and escape out the porch door."

"Thanks!" Saderia exclaimed. Then she frowned. "But why are you helping me? Did you say Dastarius was going to *kill* you if he found out about this? If that's true then why...?"

"It doesn't matter," he growled, suddenly terrified and upset again. "I'm just trying to help, so get out quickly!"

Saderia was about to say something else but at that moment the door slammed shut and she was alone with her sleeping family again. She wondered about it for just a moment before she let herself get excited. Maybe she could finally escape and be with her family, like she had always wanted!

"Mom! Dad!" she exclaimed, rushing over to their cage. "Cia! Uncle Jash! Wake up!"

Instantly the four tigers leapt to their paws and faced Saderia in her cage. They visibly relaxed when they saw she was all right but then became confused when they saw how excited she was.

"What is it?" Karenisha was the first to ask.

"It's incredible! We...!" Saderia trailed off as a horrible new truth settled over her. The slate was only in her cage, meaning the vent was only in her cage. Meaning only she could escape. Her excitement disappeared instantly to be replaced by guilt and she quickly shoved the screwdriver through the bars of her parents' cage to avoid the temptation. "Nothing," she muttered. "Never mind."

Karenisha looked at the screwdriver curiously. "Where did you get this?"

"I..." She sighed, "I don't know. Somebody gave it to me and told me that I could unscrew that slate and escape through the vents. But it's only in my cell..." She shook her head. "I'm not leaving any of you behind."

There was a long pause where Karenisha, Makero, Cia and Uncle Jash all exchanged glances and then all nodded at the same time in approval of some unspoken decision. Karenisha pushed the screwdriver back through the bars. "No, Saderia," she said sternly. "Don't worry about us. You have to go."

"No!" Saderia shouted, stopping her mother from giving her back the tool with her paw, "I can't leave you! I can't lose you again! I *won't* lose you again!"

"Saderia, stop it. Now listen to me. You have to go. You would be doing us a favor if you escaped because that could mean that you'd be better off. We'd be worried, of course, but you can do this. If you escape, it will be so much better, and we'll always be with you, in spirit."

"No." Saderia shook her head. "I won't go! You can't make me!"

"We can't," Cia agreed softly. "But you know you should go. She's right; you deserve better than this. You should be able to live out your life."

"Don't let us weigh you down," Uncle Jash agreed. "You should do what you need to do, and what you think is right."

"But I can't! I don't know if I can stand to lose you again!" Saderia gasped to her parents as tears started to drip down her face. Turning to her aunt and uncle, she exclaimed, "And I'd be losing you, too, now! I'd have no one left!"

"Saderia, this is about more than just you or me or any of us," Makero told her softly. "This is about the forest. Any good Princess or Queen or King puts their forest first and looks after it no matter what. If there's any way to stop it, we can't let Dastarius take over. You're the last of the royal family and it's up to you to save the forest."

"He's right," Karenisha agreed. "From what you've told me, I can already tell how brave you are. You're a natural-born leader, Saderia. You just have to find the confidence."

"And every good leader has to deal with loss and hard times," Makero added. "Good leaders always have to make tough decisions, but you have to look deep within yourself to make the right choice."

"The path of a Queen is a hard one," Karenisha put in. "But it is marked with experience. No matter what happens, you can know that we've been proud of you since you were first born, and we've admired your bravery and strength. We know you can do this, even though it will be hard."

Makero smiled warmly. "The forest needs someone to look up to and to turn to in times of need. It is soon, but right now, that's you, Saderia."

Saderia shook her head back and forth, tears splashing her face. "I can't do it! The forest will just have to do without me! I can't leave you here!"

Karenisha sighed. "Listen to me. We can't make

the decision for you, but we think you should do this. Life is all about taking chances. Life is lined with pain and grief but that's something you have to learn to live with. A good leader knows how to get through it and even though it might always hurt, they keep looking forward."

"Stop saying that! I'm not a good leader and I never will be! And if I leave you now, I won't be a leader, I'll be a traitor!"

"No, you won't. Just think about it. The duty of the royal family has always been to help the forest. As the royal heir, it's your duty, too."

Saderia shook her head and retreated to the far wall of her cage. She didn't want to listen to what they were saying but she couldn't help it, because it did make sense. She had always wanted to help her forest and make her parents proud of her. For a long time she had yearned to take on Queenly duties to show her aunt and uncle and the forest that she was ready. She hadn't understood how hard a Queen's job could be--until now.

She knew that she had to take responsibility and make a choice. In the time that she had been there, she had said that they couldn't let Dastarius win, but she hadn't realized that in order for him to lose, she might have to pay a price as well. She also hadn't known that the decision would be placed squarely on her shoulders.

There were a few different choices. She knew that if she stayed here, she wouldn't be helping anybody but herself, and that would make her selfish. She would just suffer here until Dastarius finally killed them, and that would do no good at all. But if she left, she might never see her parents again and they might be killed! On the other hand, they might be killed even if she didn't leave, except she might die with them. There was a slight possibility that she could somehow help her parents if she did escape since she knew the complete truth now, but she was terrified of failing. At the same time she knew that if she had any other option, she couldn't just sit around when she might be able to make a difference.

With a heavy heart she padded over to her parents' cage and gingerly took the screwdriver.

"We would have respected any choice you made," Karenisha whispered. "Good job."

Saderia nodded, trying to blink the tears out of her eyes and swallow the huge lump in her throat. Holding the screwdriver in her paw, she looked up into her parents' faces, maybe for the last time. "I'm scared," she whispered. "What if I fail?"

"Everyone's scared of failure," Makero murmured gently.

"You just have to try your hardest and do everything you can," Karenisha said softly. "Believe in yourself, Saderia. There's a lot you can do."

Saderia took a deep, ragged breath and turned to her aunt and uncle. "I'm sorry I was such a horrible niece," she muttered.

Cia was crying and she whispered, "I couldn't

have asked for a better niece, Saderia. I know you'll make the right choices."

"We all believe in you," Uncle Jash told her. "You're a very special tiger."

"Thanks," she muttered, thinking of how much she didn't deserve it. She stood still for a very long moment, staring at her family members and feeling horrible for the decision she was about to make. But she knew it was the right choice. Suddenly she felt the warmth of her parents' gaze and the kindness in her aunt and uncle's eyes. She drew in a slow, steady breath. "I'll do what I can," she murmured as she stepped over to the slate and began unscrewing it from the wall, gripping the screwdriver in her teeth stiffly.

One screw fell and hit the ground with a ping, then another, then another. The slate fell, hanging by one final screw; when it was out she caught the plate to set it to the ground.

"You'll do great, Saderia," Karenisha said.

"We love you," Makero added warmly.

Karenisha, Cia and Uncle Jash echoed the words and Saderia said them back, meaning it with all her heart and soul.

"I'll do everything I can," she corrected. She took one final look at her family before squeezing herself into the vent.

It was a very tight fit and Saderia wondered if she would be able to move at all, but she managed to ease forward. She had to keep going. She contin-

ued to squeeze herself forward, feeling very uncomfortable, and slowly made her way upward
into the main part of the air vent. It was weird to
think that, since she was underground, there must
be dirt all around her outside of the vent, except for
the part close to the house. But when she reached
the top of the vent and went forward, ignoring a
few right turns, she knew that she was above
ground and inside the house.

Beginning to feel claustrophobic, Saderia
wanted nothing more than to be out of the tiny
vent. Her legs were so stiff and cramped; she wondered if she would ever feel comfortable again. But
none of that mattered in wake of her situation and
she determinedly kept going, even though it was a
slow and unpleasant experience. Inching forward,
using her paws, she followed the directions she had
been given to keep going straight.

As she crept along the vent, she thought about
what she was doing and what she had left behind.
The sharp pain that cut through her at the thought
was enough to make her want to give up but she
persevered and kept moving. She kept herself
going by thinking about how she could possibly
get help once she was free. Of course she was
afraid of being caught and having everything left
up to her, but she had to be brave.

Finally she reached the end of the vent and in-
ched to the right in the direction, causing her body
to bend in a painful way. Gritting her teeth against
the pain of the odd angle, she pulled herself to the

right and came face to face with a grate. She peered through the metal bars and saw that beyond the grate was a dark kitchen, telling her she was in the right place. Gingerly she popped the grate out, careful not to make a sound as she slithered out of the vent, much to the relief of her cramped body.

She carefully put the grate back then stood up to look around at the kitchen, dark but nowhere near as dark as the dungeon. She wasn't safe yet, but she also wasn't ready to leave. Not without exploring first; there might be a key to the dungeon cells somewhere.

With her heart pounding in her chest, she silently slipped over to the archway separating the kitchen from the hallway. She was thankful for a moment that she *had* been in that house before and her knowledge of how to get around it might help. For a second, she stopped to think about where the likeliest place to keep the keys would be. They could be hidden somewhere in the dark living room but Dastarius might want to keep them somewhere closer to him.

She peered down the hallway at the three doors and then the doors at the end of the hall that were still locked. With a jolt, she realized that the way into the dungeon must be behind those doors; her parents were just feet away. But they were still locked up tightly. With a flash of determination, she knew that she would do anything it took to get past those doors. Then she felt confused as she remembered *how* she had escaped. The animal that had let her out had managed to get into the dungeon, but *how*? If they had the keys to the door, were they lying about not being able to find the other keys? And if that were true, then why?

She shook her head, knowing that she didn't have time for these questions and that she would just have to find her own way, leaving some mysteries for later. Recalling that Dastarius might keep the dungeon keys close to him, she padded toward the second door in the hallway after looking around. Dastarius had said that was the closet and it seemed like a place someone would keep secret keys.

When she stepped over to the closet door, it was locked but it was easy enough to pick with her claws, unlike the heavy locks on the dungeon doors and the last door. After picking the lock, she swept the hallway with her gaze then peeked inside. It was dark inside but there was no sign of Dastarius, so she quickly snuck in, closing the door quietly behind her.

Inside the closet, there were a bunch of papers, maybe even plans for their captures, and information Dastarius must have written down about the tomb and about the throne. There were several dark objects that she didn't have time to inspect. She did notice a door to the right of the closet and with a flutter of panic she realized that it must lead into Dastarius's room. She didn't dare peek at it and was very careful not to make any sound at all as she carefully inspected the entire closet, looking for something that could contain the keys.

Looking carefully, aware that not everything was as it seemed, she was able to make out a slight dent in the wall. Carefully, she used her claw to pry open a tiny secret compartment near the bottom of the floor. Her eyes gleamed with triumph as she carefully took out a tiny ring of four keys. But as soon as excitement and triumph came, doubt filled her. It couldn't be this easy, could it? The four keys looked real and she could imagine one opening the doors at the end of the hall, and the other three opening the three cells in the dungeon, but something about it seemed wrong. She had a bad feeling about it. It couldn't possibly be that easy, much as she hoped it was…could it?

She wanted to believe that it could be that simple but something inside of her was telling her otherwise and if she had learned anything from any of this, it was that she should trust her instinct. A memory flashed to the front of her mind of the words written on the front page of her mother's diary: *Trust your intuition.* She clutched the keys in despair as she struggled to make a decision. She could either trust her intuition and not try to use the keys, or she could ignore the bad feeling in her stomach. It ripped her apart, but she couldn't just ignore the feeling, much as she wanted to. She had to keep looking.

But at that moment, a light made her jump and

she had to clamp her paw over her mouth to keep from screaming. Quickly she looked around and let out a silent sigh of relief that she hadn't been caught, but it caught in her throat. She wasn't caught, but she might be soon, because the light came from the cracks in the door to Dastarius's room. Saderia froze in terror, listening intently, hearing the sound of a door opening then paw steps thudding past her hiding place and down the hall.

He was going to the dungeon! A shudder passed through her body as she thought of her poor family still down there, to be tormented. He was probably going to try to make Karenisha tell him again, but then an even scarier thought entered her mind: Once he got down there, he would see that she was gone. Then he would rush to find her, and the first place he would probably look was where the keys, real or not, were kept.

Indecision froze her in place. She had to get out of there quickly or she would be trapped again and all hope would be lost. Dastarius would somehow find out what happened and make sure it never happened again. But the thought of leaving her family behind in that horrible dungeon cut through her heart like a dagger. For a moment she argued with herself, not sure of what to do and terrified of making a mistake but after a moment she took a deep breath and calmed herself, listening to her intuition for the best choice.

With a flash of insight, she realized that she had

to escape while she could. She might be able to get around Dastarius and free her family, provided that the keys were the right ones, which she doubted, but she would have a much better chance if she got away from there now. She could always go back later, but now she had to do what she knew was best.

So when she heard the big doors leading to the dungeon slam shut and lock, she bolted out of the closet, heading for the kitchen. It broke her heart, but she didn't look back and didn't slow down as her paws thudded against the linoleum. She thrust the door to the porch open and slammed it shut behind her, heading for the screen door at the end of it. By that time, she heard a muted roar coming from the dungeon and knew that Dastarius had found out she had escaped. Terrified tears blurred her sight, but she slammed the screen door shut behind her and raced away into the dark forest without stopping or tripping.

It was still dark and Saderia guessed that Dastarius had gotten up just to torture them at that hour in the hopes that Karenisha would break and tell him. But she refused to think of her mother and father and aunt and uncle back in that disgusting dungeon as she fled through the trees without a sound except for the rustle of bushes and trees. She had never run so fast in her life, not even when she had run away from Cia and Uncle Jash. Sharp rocks tore open her paws and her sides but she did all she could not to leave a bloody path.

As she fled from the horrible place, she tripped over a large root sticking out of the ground and she half fell, biting her lip to contain a scream as her paw twisted painfully. But she caught herself and kept running, ignoring the throbbing of her badly twisted paw and the sting of branches poking into her. There was only one thing that mattered right then and that was getting away.

She knew that the first place Dastarius might look was her house but she had to get something if she was going to be on the run again. So she changed her course and charged toward her home. Her body was streaked with mud and blood by the time she reached the window of her room and crawled through it into her room without hesitation.

Homesickness welcomed her the second she stepped into her old room, looking just the way she remembered it, but she didn't hesitate as she dove under the bed and grabbed the things she had pushed under there the last time. Tightly gripping the diary and the other things in her teeth, she slipped out the window again and took off running once more in whatever direction, just determined to get far enough away that Dastarius would never find her.

She protected her precious treasured belongings as she ran, being as careful as she could in her mad retreat. Finally, another big root caught her by surprise and she fell over it onto, thankfully, a soft patch of grass where she lay panting. She had just enough energy to reach out and grab a handful of berries off one of the nearby bushes and pop them into her mouth. The food settled into her belly in a now unfamiliar way, but she felt slightly better as she faded into sleep. Her last thought was of her parents, counting on her, before she finally faded into unconsciousness.

Chapter Eleven

Hints

The first thing Saderia felt when she woke up the next morning in the now light forest was the wind rustling through her fur, and something else brushing against her face. With a groan, she opened her eyes and lifted her head, staring in awe at the sun as it shone brightly through the forest, making it sparkle with natural light. Saderia hadn't seen the beauty of sunlight in days. Around her was the cheerful chirping of birdsong, as if everything were normal, and the trees rustled gently and comfortingly in the breeze. Soft grass tickled her belly and face; only the dried blood around the small scratches in her fur and the dirt all over her remained from last night.

Absently she started licking the blood away and cleaning the dirt off of her, wondering what she was supposed to be doing. The situation from last night and all that she had learned came rushing back to her. It felt as if a dagger were being drove into her heart as she thought of how she had abandoned her family. She closed her eyes, trying to block out the severe pain, but rethought it and instead faced the pain bravely. She had left them for a reason: to help them. And she was going to do everything she could to make sure that what she had done hadn't been a mistake.

But there was a problem and that was that Saderia didn't know where to begin. The first thought that crossed her mind, of course, was to go back to Dastarius's dungeon and free her parents with the keys she had taken from the closet. They could be the right ones and it was the only thing she had to go on at that time.

But at the exact moment the thought crossed her mind, a breeze blew a strange piece of paper into her face. With a surprised hiss, she pulled the paper away from her face and her eyes widened even before she read it. It had obviously been torn from her mother's diary, which was lying open beside her, unlike last night. One of the pens that she had grabbed lay to the side, as if it had been used but the rest of her things were undisturbed, including Dastarius's keys.

Her confusion and shock only grew as she gazed at the piece of paper, her amber eyes widening as she read the words scribbled across the page. The words read:

Don't go back! Too many guards! They're safe! Go to an old cabin in the woods far west of Dastarius's house for help. It's covered by vines and hidden behind trees, but it's by a tree struck by lightning. You have the wrong keys. The right keys are in the cabin.

Sarah Renée

Saderia stared at the note in wonder. The handwriting was unfamiliar but she had a sinking suspicion that the same animal who had helped her escape had somehow managed to find her and had written this note. Again she wondered why they were helping her, but she had more important things to think about. She didn't think it was a trap only because of who she suspected had written it. It was obvious that whoever was doing this was trying to help her, and she had thought there was something strange and too simple about the keys she had found. It seemed the keys *were* some sort of trap!

But what about the cabin in the note? What did it have to do with her situation and what help could it possibly give her? It made no sense, but something was telling her to trust whoever had written the note to help her. Besides, it was the only thing she had to go on because she didn't think she could go back. As soon as she thought it, she realized how true it was. Dastarius was smart, and he wouldn't have chased after her; that wasn't what he was doing now. He was at home, waiting for her to return for her parents because he knew she would. Saderia knew that was his plan and she wasn't going to walk right into it.

She looked back at the note, overwhelmed with relief when she realized that the 'they' in the note most likely meant her family. With all her heart, she hoped the note was right and they were safe, and she also hoped it wasn't another trap. But it couldn't be a trap. If someone who was trying to hurt her had found her to write the note, wouldn't they have just taken her instead of setting up some trap? She did wonder how the note-writer had known these things but decided not to question it because there were always new ways of getting information, and if the animal who wrote this knew more now than when he had helped her escape, that was hardly suspicious.

She studied the note carefully, trying to figure out where to go. She knew which way must be west of Dastarius's home and could probably get there without getting close to the house where Dastarius and his minions would be waiting to grab her. Quickly judging where she was and how long it would take her to get to the west side of Dastarius's home without actually getting close to it, she tucked the note into her diary, stuffed the rest of her belongings, including the keys, into it then took off into the forest, clutching it tightly in her jaws.

This time was much easier since she wasn't fleeing from anybody and she regained her agility to maneuver her way through the forest without getting hurt or tripped up. She ducked under branches and leapt over roots, feeling the smooth grass under her sore paws. As she ran she plucked berries off bushes she passed and popped them into her mouth to ease the hunger she had felt for days. The food felt strange in her belly but it would keep her strength up and she ate every chance she got, liking the cool taste of berry juice on her tongue.

Finally she stopped to judge where she was and realized she had reached her destination. Now she just had to find the strange cabin mentioned in the note. She easily picked out which way was west and began fast walking through the bushes, keeping a sharp eye out for the landmark she had been given. At first she hadn't thought finding a lightning-stricken tree would be too hard because of its conspicuousness. But in this part of the forest where all the trees were squished together, making it hard to get around, she couldn't make out anything. The canopy of leaves overhead blocked out the sun and only a few patches of sunlight escaped through it. But she didn't let that faze her and kept going.

It was quiet in that part of the woods; she only heard the muted sound of birdsong occasionally, as if it were far away. This part of the woods was overgrown with weeds and vines and the trees were covered with green fungi. The trees had thick branches and Saderia had to squeeze between them to see where she was going. Because of the darkness and closeness of trees, finding one tree struck by lightning was no easy task and Saderia wandered around for a long time, searching for it.

Eventually she stopped, frustrated, and tried to think of a better way to find that particular tree.

She was beginning to think maybe it didn't exist at all or she was in the wrong part of the forest, but didn't want to give up too soon. Suddenly an idea came to her. She hurried over to one of the thick oaks growing in that woods and gently placed her belongings under one of the big roots so they wouldn't be disturbed.

Then she tilted her head to look up to the top of the big oak, yards above her, and jumped at the tree, claws outstretched. As soon as her claws dug through the bark, she pushed herself upward and kept herself from falling by hooking her claws into the bark. As she got higher it got easier because she could grab onto one of the branches then jump to the next one. By doing that, she finally managed to climb to the very top of the oak where she poked her head up through the leafy branches to look out at her forest.

Her mouth opened in wonder as she took in the view; it was the most amazing thing she had ever seen. She hadn't realized just how far up the oak was, and from this vantage point, she could look out over her whole forest. She could see her den far away, situated in a clump of thick woods, though not nearly as thick as the woods she was in now. She could see towns filled with animals going about their daily routine or fretting about her pro-longed absence. She could see neighborhoods filled with animals coming out of their houses to greet each other and share news. She could see every tree, every dip and every hill in her forest.

The scene was so peaceful and empowering it took her breath away. She watched as a gentle wind rustled the landscape of her forest, the rustling sound ringing in her ears. It was a beautiful yet fragile thing, and she felt the power of it fill her tired limbs with new strength. She actually felt herself smiling as she drank in the warmth of the scene.

Knowing she had a mission to complete, she ducked her head back down under the leaves so that only the woods she was in was visible. It was still a breathtaking sight because she could see everything in the green woods from there. With a flash of excitement, her eyes drifted to a charred tree, very precisely split in half. A lightning-stricken tree.

Saderia quickly judged where it was, what direction she should go when she got down and approximately how long it would take to get there, before leaping down the branches and then clawing her way back down the tree to leap to the ground when she was close enough. She briskly grabbed the diary, the keys and the note and took off running in the right direction. She let herself get excited when she ran into the lightning tree and immediately began searching for the cabin that was supposed to be there. It took her a while to find it only because it was covered, like the trees, with green fungus, and draped with vines, overgrown shrubs, and lower trees. But eventually she found a creaky staircase leading up to a dark cabin.

She found a rusty door and as she sat back and grabbed the handle, she didn't know what to expect. But before she pulled on the handle, she noticed that it was locked and required a key. Despair wrapped around her but almost instantaneously she shrugged it off and dropped the diary. She opened it and took out Dastarius's keys hopefully. Her intuition was telling her to try it so she carefully put the first key into the lock and turned it. Having no luck, she tried the second key and heard the lock click.

Surprised, she opened the door with a rusty creak, still not knowing what she should expect to be inside. The last thing she would have suspected was exactly what she saw. When she opened the door she was instantly greeted by the wails and cries of children. Her eyes widened in shock as she stepped in and looked around at the inside of the cabin.

The walls were old and dirty, made of wood like the outside of the old shack. But there were bars stretching across the length of the cabin right in front of her, and concealed within those cages were children!

"Who are you?" moaned a panther who looked about five.

Saderia could only stare at them for a very long time, wondering what she had walked into.

A little lion was crying and a tiger who looked

to be six stepped up to the bars, glaring but seeming confused.

"You're not that lion, so who are you?" the tiger asked.

Saderia stared for a moment longer but jumped as the cub's words sank in. "Lion?" she stammered. "What lion?" She stepped closer to the bars, seeing how dirty and sad all of the children looked and wondering what she could possibly do to help them. Why were they there in the first place?

"That evil one," a tiny jaguar answered her.

"Yeah," the tiger agreed. "He has a black mane and dark brown fur. He's mean!"

"Dastarius!" Saderia exclaimed as understanding hit her.

"Yeah, I think that's his name," a lion said.

"What...what are you doing in there?" Saderia stammered, pressing up against the bars. "Who are all of you and how'd you get here?"

"That lion put us here," the tiger replied. "I'm Kachita."

"I'm Learo," said the lion.

"I'm Kasa," the jaguar told her.

"My name's Tarque," the panther added. "And Kachita's right. That lion put us here."

"We miss our parents," Learo put in quietly.

"How long have you been here?" Saderia asked.

"A long time," Kachita told her.

Learo, Kasa, Tarque and the other children nodded. There were a lot of them, almost twenty.

"Who are *you*?" Tarque asked her.

"P-princess Saderia," she murmured, still shocked. Some pieces were starting to fit together and she was stunned.

Kasa beamed. "The *Princess*?! Wow!"

"Did you come to save us?" Kachita asked hopefully.

"I...I can try..." Saderia was still stunned. "I don't know how but..." Suddenly she saw the lock on the cage and remembered what had opened the door of the cabin. Suddenly it all fit together and she figured out why she had been told to come here and why Dastarius had put the children in here.

The children in front of her had to be the ones that had been kidnapped, the ones Cia and Uncle Jash had told her about so long ago! And now she knew that Dastarius had kidnapped them, probably to get their parents to turn their backs on Cia and Uncle Jash when they couldn't help them. Once that happened, Dastarius would have promised them he could find their children somehow, since he knew exactly where they were. The animals, not knowing he was the kidnapper, would have desperately turned to him and did whatever he told them to do. It all made sense!

Now she knew why the note had told her to go here for help. And she knew she *could* help.

"Hang on," Saderia said quickly, pulling Dastarius's keys out and sprinting over to the lock. "I'll get you out in just a second." She tried the first key, then the third and the lock clicked. Saderia yanked open the cage door and all the children cheered as they poured out of the cage. "Don't go anywhere!" Saderia warned. "We're still a long way from civilization."

They all stayed in place and waited for her to lead them home. Saderia was about to take them to town, because once their children were back, Dastarius's minions wouldn't listen to him and she wouldn't have to worry about that part. But she still needed the keys to the dungeon where her family was being kept and as she wondered where she would find them, she caught sight of the note once more and her eyes widened as she read the part about the keys again.

If Dastarius's keys opened things in here, there were still two more places to be unlocked and according to the note, they could hold exactly what she was looking for.

"Are you coming?" Kasa asked her, tipping her head to one side in confusion.

"One minute," Saderia mumbled. She turned to the children. "Did any of you find any keys when you were in there?"

The children all looked at each other and all of them shook their head no.

"We *did* find a door!" Kachita told her.

"Yeah," Learo agreed. "But it was locked."

"We hoped we could escape from it," Tarque put in. "But Learo's right, it's locked."

"Thanks," Saderia muttered. "I think I can unlock it. Where is it?"

"It's over here," Kachita told her. "It's really hidden but we've been here for a long time so we found it!"

The little tiger led her into the cage and over to one wall. There was a little, old empty dresser in front of her when she stopped but she pushed it a little out of the way and revealed a door molded into the wall like the ones Saderia had gotten used to seeing. Sure enough, it was locked, but Saderia opened it with the fourth of Dastarius's keys.

"Thanks," she mumbled to Kachita as she stepped inside. "Wait for just a minute, then I'll take you home."

"Okay," Kachita said, stepping over to the other children again.

Saderia stepped through the door to an old room cluttered with old, faded objects that she couldn't name. At one point it might have been used by somebody to store things or maybe even live in, but that was obviously a long time ago by the looks of the place. But she knew that what she saw couldn't be all that was there, and she carefully groped along the walls until she finally found what she had been looking for: a tiny secret compartment at the very bottom of the far left wall. It had taken her three sweeps of the room to find it because it was very well hidden but Saderia knew what to look for and she wasn't leaving until she found it.

Carefully she used the first of Dastarius's keys to unlock the little compartment and opened it like a drawer to reveal a ring of three keys. Saderia grabbed them and held onto them like they were precious gold. To her, they were much, much better than gold, and she held them tightly as she bolted from the room and the cage to join the children.

"Did you find what you wanted?" Learo asked.

Saderia nodded, grinning. "I did." She breathed a sigh of relief. "I think everything's going to be okay. Now come on, let's get you all home."

She gently stuck the keys in her diary and quickly began leading the group of children away through the forest, back to town.

"Know where we are?" Saderia asked the children.

"Yeah!" a few of them exclaimed.

"I can see my Mom!" a few others cried out happily, running out to meet some of the animals in the town.

As soon as the animals saw their missing children, they froze, then rushed toward them, hugging them, asking them where they'd been and crying all at the same time. Saderia's heart hurt as she wished she could run to her parents and be welcomed like that, but she had a few tasks to do first.

"Come on," Saderia told the remaining children. "We'll find your parents, too, so don't worry. Stick close to me but feel free to go if you see your Mom or Dad."

A few of the parents who were clinging to their

children looked up. "Princess Saderia?!" a parent gasped, one that was holding onto Learo as if she would never let him go ever again.

Saderia dipped her head to all of them. "Greetings," she said as calmly as she could.

Another of the parents, gripping one of the younger children stared at her wide-eyed with gratitude. "You brought them back?"

Saderia nodded. "I did what any good leader should do."

"Yeah!" Kasa spoke up from her mother's arms. "She came into this shack we were in and she rescued us! She had these weird keys and then she found something and she brought us here!"

"She's a hero!" another of the children exclaimed.

"She certainly is," a mother murmured.

Another parent staggered over to her. "Thank you so much," she whispered. "We've missed them terribly."

Saderia nodded with a kind smile. "Anything to help my forest."

The mothers clustered around her, thanking her over and over with undying gratitude, warmth bringing tears to their eyes.

"I was just doing what I had to," Saderia finally told them. "Dastarius kidnapped them…"

Some of them gasped and murmuring broke out.

"Yes, it was him," Saderia told them. "He

tricked you."

"And he used our husbands to attack you...I'm so sorry, Princess Saderia!" one of the mothers said and the others took up the apology.

Saderia waved away their apologies. "No worries. It's all working out. But I think now would be a good time to go get your husband's to tell them the good news."

Most of the mothers hurried off with their children, thanking her one last time, but Kasa's mother stayed.

"You've got more to do, don't you?" she asked, knowingly.

Saderia nodded. "You don't know the half of it."

"Then let me make it a little easier for you. I can take the other children back to their mothers and get their fathers. I know all of their parents."

Saderia hesitated. "Well, I don't know..."

"You can trust me," she insisted. "I'll get them home safely."

"Yeah, she's really nice!" Kachita, one of the remaining children, spoke up.

A few of the other children added their approval as well, and Saderia made up her mind.

"Thank you," she said warmly to Kasa's mother. "I'd really appreciate the help."

Kasa's mother smiled back at her. "I'll be sure to tell them all that you saved the children." Then her face darkened. "What are you going to do about Dastarius?"

Saderia sucked in a breath but faced the mother calmly. "Just leave him to me."

The mother nodded seriously and led the children away into another part of the forest. Saderia watched them go. She hoped all their parents would be happy at finding their children again, and maybe enough animals would know the truth about Dastarius to stop him from taking over. And several animals had seen her alive, too, and that would definitely mess with his plans. But he didn't know about that *yet* and he still had her parents. Besides, he might think that if he had the Power, it wouldn't matter anymore.

Fear wrapped around her when she thought of what he might do to her family when he found all of this out, but she couldn't let herself get so scared. She had to be strong and smart about what she could do, and she knew that it would do no good to go charging into that house now, when there were still a bunch of guards.

Her plan was to wait until night; by that time all of the guards would know that their children were back, and with any luck, Dastarius would be asleep so she could just sneak into the house, get her family and run. But it wasn't that simple either, because she only had three keys, one for each cell. Dastarius must have the key that opened the door on the end of the hall that led to the dungeon. How would she be able to take it from him? Would she have to *fight* him to get it? She would like nothing more than to sink her claws into that evil lion but she shied away from the idea because she doubted she could win. But then again, she would do whatever it took to help her family.

That night, Dastarius went down to the dungeon one final time. Saderia might have escaped, and he didn't know how it was possible, but he might be able to use it to his advantage.

"What do you want?" Karenisha hissed as he stepped down into the dungeon beside their cage. Ever since Saderia had gone, she and Makero had not stopped worrying about their daughter. They had no way of knowing if she had gotten out at all or if she were safe. They didn't even know if she was alive! They tried to have hope that she was strong enough to make it out and find a way to help, even, but they couldn't hide their doubts.

"Get out of here," Cia hissed at him. She and Jash had been just as terrified and they couldn't get rid of their uncertainty that Saderia had made it. There were just so many obstacles and they knew that Dastarius had brought his guards to capture Saderia if she returned. They hoped she had stayed away, but had no way of knowing and that was the worst thing about their situation.

Dastarius ignored Cia and turned to Karenisha. "Lose something?" he taunted.

"Saderia is safe and you'll never get her!" Karenisha growled.

"How can you be so sure?" Dastarius asked,

grinning triumphantly. "How do you know my plan didn't work? That she was too caught up worrying about you that she came back here, and got caught by my guards?"

"Leave her alone," Makero snarled as Karenisha took a step backward, trying not to show him how terrified she was.

"I would know because then she'd be down here," Karenisha said carefully, not believing her own words.

Dastarius sneered at her. "And if I don't allow her the privilege of seeing her family one last time? If I've got her somewhere else?"

Karenisha took another step backward, fear for her daughter blocking out everything else. She didn't want to believe it, but what if he was telling the truth? If Saderia had gotten out of the dungeon, wouldn't he try another one just to be on the safe side? And he really was cruel enough to keep her away from her family...to torture her...to torture Karenisha.

"What do you mean by 'one last time?'" Cia asked nervously, seeming just as horrified as Karenisha.

Panic and dismay nearly stopped Karenisha's heart as she read the meaning in his words. "You can't!" she gasped without thinking.

Dastarius's grin grew even wickeder. "Of course I can." His gaze darkened then and he glared at Karenisha hatefully. "I'm done with this stupid game. If you don't tell me how to get that scroll, I will kill your daughter as painfully as necessary."

"Stay away from her!" Makero roared, trying in vain to break the bars of his cage.

Dastarius glared at him coldly, triumph lighting up his eyes. "What can you do? Nothing. I, on the other hand, can guarantee you that Saderia will feel a lot of pain before she dies if you don't tell me what I want right now."

"You don't have her!" Karenisha shouted. "You *can't* have her!"

"But I do."

"No...!"

"Let's think about this for a moment, Karenisha. No matter how much you may want to believe I don't have her, you know there's a chance that I *do*. Are you really willing to risk your daughter's life for an old piece of paper?"

Karenisha gritted her teeth and stayed silent for a long time, looking down. The silence lengthened then Karenisha took a deep breath and, without looking up, muttered, "It's behind our house, to the right. Keep going right for about half an hour if you're walking and then take another right until you find it. It's covered with bushes and vines."

"Karenisha!" Makero exclaimed.

"It's not worth it!" Karenisha shouted back. Her eyes were full of pain and suffering.

Cia and Jash could only watch in silence, not sure of what to do.

Dastarius's eyes glittered. "And the code?"

Karenisha closed her eyes and took a deep breath. "Heart, crown, scepter, eye, and then the picture that looks like a fluffy cloud."

"Finally!" Dastarius exclaimed triumphantly.

"Okay, you have the code, now give us our daughter back," Makero snarled.

Dastarius smirked at him. "I'll give you your daughter back when I find out whether or not you're lying."

He turned but before he could leave, Karenisha shouted, "What are you doing anyway? What makes you think you'll be King, even *with* the Power?"

He turned back around with a triumphant sneer. "Since you're going to die, I suppose it can't hurt to let you in on my plan. First of all, it was I who kidnapped the children and messed with the forest to cause desperation so that the forest would trust me and turn on Cia and Jash." Cia and Jash snarled at him but he ignored them and went on, "Then I would be the one to return the children and help everyone, unlike the King and Queen, so I would be the hero and they would trust me. Karenisha, Makero, so sorry to have to tell you, but when I get my Power, you'll die. And then so will Saderia, and I'll make it look like Cia and Jash did it because they wanted the throne which would be why they killed Karenisha and Makero, and then Saderia because she found out. Then they'll be run out of town and *I* will be King because of all I've done to help them, and because I have the Power."

Karenisha let out a growl of shock as the plan came together in her mind and Makero snarled at him, clawing at the cage, but it was no use. Dastarius gave them one last haughty glance and then without another word, he turned around and raced up the stairs as fast as he could, not bothering to shut the door behind him in his race to get to the tomb.

Behind him Karenisha and Makero shouted at him to bring Saderia back to them but it was no use.

Saderia silently padded through the dark woods, loving the cover of night as she made her way to Dastarius's house. Her heart was pounding wildly with fear but she ignored it, thinking only about freeing her parents. But she knew she would have to be careful and couldn't just leap into the situation.

She had come up with another solution in case she couldn't find the keys that led to the door at the end of the hall. Her fallback plan was that she could crawl back through the vents and unlock her cage from inside and then her parents' cages. Then maybe the door wouldn't be locked from the inside and they could escape from there, or if worse came to worse, they might even be able to squeeze into the vent.

She had come with only the keys from the cabin

to unlock the dungeon's cages, leaving her mother's diary and the other keys back at her house, hoping she'd be able to return for them later. Right then, they'd only slow her down. Gripping the ring of keys tightly in her jaws, she padded silently toward Dastarius's house, alert for any movement that could give away an approaching attacker.

By this time she was sure all of the animals had heard that their children were back and had left the house but she was careful anyway. Besides, she still had to keep her eyes open for Dastarius.

She stalked forward, ready to attempt to pick the lock on the front door but she was surprised to find that it had carelessly been left open. Wondering if this were some sort of trick, she stepped inside the dark house cautiously, slipping unnoticeably through the living room. She poked her head through the archway and, seeing no one, crept down the short stretch of hall, pressing close to the wall. She peered around the corner at the other hall and was relieved to find that it, too, was empty.

But then she saw something even more amazing: the door at the end of the hall was *open*! She was about to rush toward it, excitement pulsing inside her, but then she stopped, again wondering if there was a trap. She thought about it for a long moment and came to the conclusion that it wasn't a trap, but there was something wrong here. Padding slowly down the hall, she was even brave enough to look under the door to Dastarius's room. He wasn't there, which scared Saderia. Could he be down in the dungeon right now?

As she wondered about what she should do, she knew she wouldn't get another chance like this, where the escape route was so clear. If these keys opened the cells, then she could hold off Dastarius long enough to free her family if he were down there. With her family free, the five of them could probably defeat him, or at least escape. This seemed like a good idea, so she ran for the open door and paused in the doorway.

In front of her was an L-shaped hallway that led to a room at the corner of it. The door leading into that room was open and she guessed it led to the dungeon so ran for it. But when she reached that door she paused because she saw another door at the end of the hall to the right. She wanted to check it out but ignored the curiosity of that room and kept going.

Inside the corner room it was dark but she saw an open door on the back wall. Even from there she could tell that there was a staircase behind it. Her excitement mingled with fear as she raced toward the door and began slipping down the stairs, wanting to take Dastarius by surprise if he were down there instead of announcing her arrival like an idiot.

But as she slipped down the stairs, she realized that Dastarius was nowhere to be seen in the little dungeon. She was confused on top of relieved but raced the rest of the way down the stairs, calling,

"Mom! Dad! Cia! Uncle Jash!"

When she reached the bottom of the stairs and rushed to their cages, she saw Karenisha and Makero's eyes widen with surprise, fear and relief, all in one.

"Saderia?!" they both gasped at the same time.

"What are you doing here?!" Cia and Uncle Jash exclaimed from their cell.

"I have the keys!" Saderia shouted excitedly. "I can free you!"

Without giving them a chance to reply, she jammed the second key into Karenisha and Makero's cell lock and yanked open the door. "You're free!"

Their mouths dropped open and for a moment they were frozen to the spot, faced with the foreign concept of freedom. But then they raced out of the cell as fast as they could and huddled against the far wall of the dungeon, still wide-eyed and open-mouthed with shock. But Saderia could see excitement glittering in their amber and green eyes. The only thing that bothered her was that the gleam was dulled by terror and horror, and she couldn't understand why, if they were finally free.

Not stopping to think about it, she moved to Cia and Uncle Jash's cage and unlocked it with the third key.

"Thank goodness!" Cia exclaimed, bolting out of the cage with Uncle Jash right behind her.

"We have to get out of here!" Saderia exclaimed. "Before Dastarius gets back!"

"Um, Saderia..." Karenisha murmured hesitantly. "I don't think you'll have to worry about Dastarius being back for a while."

Saderia turned to her suspiciously. "Why not?"

There was a long silence and then Karenisha murmured, "Because I told him how to get into the tomb."

Chapter Twelve

Power Struggle

Saderia stood speechless for a moment, unsure of how to respond. "How...how could you tell him...?" She trailed off because it didn't matter, not anymore. What mattered was whether or not they could stop him and set things right. She shook her head, quickly saying, "Never mind! We have to get to that tomb and stop him!"

Without waiting for their consent, Saderia took off running up the stairs with her parents and aunt and uncle hard on her heels. All of them looked surprised at the house above their jail, how ordinary-looking it seemed when it had housed such a monster, and how easily she made her way through it. But Saderia didn't stop to explain everything to them and instead led them out of the doors, down the hall, through the living room and finally out the front door.

She kept running, knowing where to go from the time when she had accidentally stumbled onto her oldest ancestor's tomb, but Karenisha and Makero froze behind her in shock. Saderia skidded to a halt and whirled around to face them, ready to rebuke them for slowing them down but the words died in her throat when she saw the way her mother and father were looking at the outside world the way it should have been treated: as a miracle, the way only prisoners would see it.

They said nothing because there were probably no words for the feelings and the awe inspired by finally seeing the outside world again. Unconsciously, Karenisha brushed her paw across the grass, it's soft touch unfamiliar after coming from the awful dungeon. They jumped when the trees rustled then stood absolutely still, as if any movement might shatter this beautiful dream and they'd find themselves locked up in the cellar again.

"Karenisha?" Cia asked, worriedly stepping closer to her sister. Cia and Uncle Jash were a little surprised at how much grander the world seemed when it had been taken away from them, but they hadn't been locked away for as long as her parents.

"Makero?" Uncle Jash echoed Cia's concern as he stepped over to him.

Karenisha blinked and she and Makero exchanged a glance. "We're all right," she murmured, her voice breathless sounding. "We've just been underground for a long time."

Makero nodded, awe-struck. "How does it look in daylight?"

"Beautiful," Saderia replied. "I understand what you're feeling completely." As she said it she thought of the amazing view she had gotten from the top of the oak and smiled to herself, but instantly returned to seriousness. "And I understand how amazing and strange this all must seem, but I don't think we have much time. We have to stop Dastarius."

They shook themselves. "Right," Makero agreed.

"But, um, I know the directions to the tomb but I don't know the way around the forest anymore," Karenisha said unhappily.

"That's all right," Saderia assured them. "I know the way to the tomb; I've been there before."

Karenisha's eyes popped open. "You have?!"

Saderia nodded. "I found it by accident. Now, come on!" Giving them no more time to get used to the natural world, she took off into the trees and her family followed close behind her.

Saderia knew that no matter how urgent this was, she needed to take care of her family, too, and she would hate herself if she didn't. When she caught sight of delicious berries growing on a nearby bush, she grabbed them off the branch and presented them to Karenisha, Makero, Cia and Uncle Jash.

"Eat, you need your strength," she instructed them.

Immediately Cia and Uncle Jash began to nibble up the berries and Saderia tried to hide her surprise at how they had listened to her so easily. Karenisha and Makero dropped down to sniff the berries in front of them before hesitantly putting one into their mouths. Both of them looked surprised as the unfamiliar cool, refreshing berry juice seeped into their mouths and they quickly swallowed more of them.

Karenisha, now more confident and looking more like the regal Queen she must have once been, stood up determinedly. "It's getting easier. I think I can remember all this now." She leveled her gaze with her daughter's. "Lead the way. We have to end this."

Saderia's paws thudded against the ground, and she was flanked on both sides by her parents, both of them running through the forest easily as everything they remembered about the glorious outside world came back to them. Even if they were still confused and a little afraid, they were careful not to show it, acting like the King and Queen Saderia knew they had been.

Cia and Uncle Jash were right behind them, following Saderia as she led them through the woods, back to their home. Karenisha and Makero looked a little overwhelmed at the thought of getting their freedom, their family and their home back all at once, but in a good way. As they crashed through the bushes and trampled the light grass under their paws, Saderia turned to her parents, giving them a curious but not angry look.

"Now might be a good time to tell me why you told him where the tomb was, Mom," she said carefully.

Karenisha winced in pain, even though she had agilely avoided a sharp stick in her path. "I didn't know what happened to you after you escaped," she said quietly, keeping pace while speaking.

"None of us did," Cia put in, while Uncle Jash made a sound of agreement.

"It was devastating, not knowing," Makero added grimly.

"Dastarius came down to the dungeon right before you came back," Karenisha explained. "He told us he had recaptured you because you had come right back, in hopes of freeing us. I believed him, because I thought that you might, well, do what he said you had."

"I almost did," Saderia agreed sympathetically.

Karenisha let out a sharp breath of air. "I'm so glad you didn't."

"So Dastarius came down and threatened you with my life," she guessed.

Karenisha squeezed her eyes shut for a brief second before opening them just in time to dodge over a big root in their path, her leap graceful and smooth as she jumped at the same time Saderia and Makero did, a family tuned it to each other completely. "Yes," she murmured, "I didn't know what else to do. If he did have you, I couldn't just let him take your life. You haven't even had much time to live it!"

Makero let out a sad sigh while Cia and Uncle Jash exchanged guilt-ridden glances.

"So I did the only thing I could: tell him," Karenisha muttered. "I felt so helpless."

"We all did," Makero murmured as they raced through the green blur of the forest around them.

He turned to his daughter with curiosity sparkling in his green eyes. "How did you find the keys to free us, and how did you get past the guards and everything?"

Karenisha looked at Saderia then, too, with a mixture of wonder and awe. "Yes, how did you do it?"

Cia and Uncle Jash turned their questioning glances on their niece as well, and Uncle Jash murmured, "I'm wondering that too. I thought I'd never see the light of day again."

Saderia judged where they were and tried to estimate how long it would take them to reach the tomb. Deciding she had enough time, she delved into the tale that had led to her parents' freedom as they raced along the forest floor, all of them headed to a hopefully better future together.

She had their undivided attention as she recounted her experience while searching for a way to help her family, who she cared about more than anything. She noticed, as she was telling her tale, that Cia and Uncle Jash were awed outside listeners. But Karenisha and Makero felt in her emotions almost exactly as if it were happening to all three of them at that very moment, as if they knew exactly how she had felt without her having to tell them what impact the events had had on her.

"So Dastarius was the kidnapper..." Cia muttered, looking stunned by all that she had come to know in just a few short days.

Uncle Jash shook his head, his eyes wide.

"Nothing will be the same after this." He turned to look at Saderia and a ghost of a grin lit up his face. "And that's a promise, Saderia."

Saderia beamed back at him, reading into the words. He believed they would be able to get through whatever the next obstacle was as a family, and then things would be different, and not just in terms of her parents being back. If they could survive the next ordeal, she might finally have a voice. She was still afraid, though, that she would fail or do something to jeopardize that nice vision of the future. After all, it wasn't over yet.

But then Karenisha turned to her with a smile that could light up the entire forest. "I told you that you could do it," she said warmly.

Saderia couldn't help but beam back at her, pride flowing through her body and giving her new strength and determination. She told them the end of her story, of how confused she was when she went back to Dastarius's house and found all the doors open, no need for any other key she might have had to fight for.

"He was excited that he finally got what he wanted," Karenisha muttered bitterly. "He must not have cared about that anymore. He probably thought that nothing could stop him after that."

Saderia narrowed her eyes. "We'll soon see about that."

Makero nodded, his mouth an angry line but his eyes gleaming. "Yes, we will!"

Cia was about to say something but suddenly Karenisha shushed her by saying, "I think we're getting closer; we should be sneakier."

Saderia and the rest of her family slowed to slip through the forest, using trees and bushes as cover and barely making a sound to alert Dastarius to their presence if he were there.

"I'll take a look," Saderia hissed, and crept toward where she had seen the tomb before anyone could stop her. She pushed through a thick clump of brush and ducked under a low branch and then snuck over to a huge bush to hide in, peeking through the other side to the area where she knew the tomb was located.

The leafy bush around her rustled softly with her sharp intake of breath as she saw Dastarius excitedly standing over the ancient stone slab protecting the tomb of her oldest ancestor. But the tomb wouldn't be a mystery for much longer because Dastarius instantly located the code lock and began to turn the little blocks of wood to the correct pictures.

Saderia signaled for her family to join her with a flick of her tail and in a matter of moments, her mother and father were crouched in the bush beside her, while Cia and Uncle Jash hid in another clump of brush beside them.

"Now?" she asked.

Karenisha nodded, unsheathing and flexing her claws while Makero tore up the ground. Her mother shot her father a nervous glance that actually reassured Saderia more than worried her; at least she wasn't the only one that was afraid. Her father's face was angry and determined and through gritted teeth, he growled, "There are five of us and one of him. We can do this."

Saderia knew it was true and the odds were in their favor. She and her family had stopped at every berry bush to eat and had their strength returned to them as a result, so they would not be so easily overpowered. Her body still felt weak with fear and tension but she flexed her muscles and sunk her claws into the ground. In the next bush, she saw Cia and Uncle Jash preparing for a fight and looking at them for the cue to strike.

"Now," Karenisha hissed and all five of them surged out of the bushes, heading toward Dastarius with a ferocious snarl. But the evil lion hardly noticed them because at that moment he slipped the last picture into its correct place and, very slowly, the slate began to slide away from the tomb, causing the earth to tremble around it with the effort.

The five of them skidded to a halt behind Dastarius as they watched the slate slide away and begin to reveal the tomb.

"What's happening?" Cia exclaimed.

Neither Karenisha nor Makero bothered to answer, too busy staring at the moving slate with horror and awe.

"No!" Saderia cried.

For the first time, Dastarius whirled around and saw them. For a moment a look of panic crossed his face but it was gone in an instant and he sneered at them as the tomb continued to open itself. "You're too late!" he announced as he turned back around and squeezed his way into the tomb, now that there was a crack between the slate and what lie underneath it.

Saderia let out a gasp and hurried forward to look into the dark depths of the tomb as the slate stopped moving, giving them enough room to enter it. Feeling light-headed at the thought of entering a thousand-year-old tomb and facing Dastarius at the same time, she stepped back as her eyes adjusted to the blackness beneath to make out a dusty old staircase.

But at that moment she shrugged off her fear and bravely slipped into the tomb as the slate began to move back, about to seal the tomb once more. Unhesitatingly, she dived through the crack; she was just small enough to make it through. She began racing quickly but not recklessly down the staircase as there was a crash above her, marking the resealing of the tomb. It didn't matter that she was trembling so badly that she could barely stop herself from stumbling, and it didn't matter that she wanted to be anywhere but there. Dastarius was endangering *her* forest, and *her* family. He had already destroyed her life and snatched her parents away from her for ten years. She wasn't going to let him win again, no matter what it took!

She heard alarmed shouts from above as her family tried desperately to reopen the tomb but she didn't slow down as she swept down the seemingly endless flight of stairs. She couldn't see Dastarius; he blended into the blackness all too well, but she knew he must be somewhere up ahead, and moments later she heard an exclamation of excitement.

Knowing that Dastarius had reached the end of the stairs and only being able to imagine what he was seeing, she picked up her pace until she almost tumbled over the last step, nearly landing face-first on the smooth, cool stone that lined the tomb beneath her. She stood up, shivering, fearfully aware that she was in the burial place of her oldest ancestor, the one who had started the royal family. She hoped that Queen Tarae, wherever she may be, wouldn't find any disrespect in what was about to take place in her tomb.

As she struggled to her paws, she looked around and her breath caught in her throat. Not dulled by the dimness of the light were piles and piles of gold lining the first part of the tomb. There were amulets and jewelry, golden jugs and scepters; all of it glittered faintly but enticingly and there wasn't a spot in the room that wasn't filled with gold or relics from her ancestor's life. Saderia could sense the feeling and love behind all those treasures and recalled how the forest had loved Queen Tarae's intelligent ruling. The animals of long, long ago must have greatly respected Queen Tarae and given her such a great tomb as a way to thank her for what she had done and to remember her. A dark archway led into a room that she couldn't yet see into. But standing in front of that archway, Saderia was able to make out a shape against the darkness when her eyes adjusted enough.

Dastarius was standing in the middle of her ancestor's precious gold and belongings, reveling in its richness as if it belonged entirely to him. He was hard to make out, his mane black on black and his dark brown fur just as dark and hard to see. But she could see the triumphant, evilly excited gleam of his amber eyes glowing in the blackness.

"Dastarius!" she hissed, taking a step toward him. She narrowed her amber eyes, certain that was all he could clearly see of her as well. She snarled at him. "This isn't your treasure. It belongs to Queen Tarae alone, not you or anyone! Get out of her burial place!"

Dastarius's eyes widened in surprise as he whirled around to see her but then narrowed and his exposed fangs gleamed. "Your words are meaningless now! The forest is mine, the Power is mine! What can you do to stop me?!"

"Have you no respect for the dead?" Saderia snapped. She answered herself. "No, all you care about is yourself!" She glared at him. "But I'll show you what I intend to do to stop you!"

She lunged at Dastarius, claws outstretched but

Dastarius jumped out of her way and she crashed into a wall of gold, thankfully damaging neither her or the gold. Leaping up to snarl at Dastarius, she prepared to attack, and Dastarius met her glare with a furious snarl, but then he froze, staring through the archway into the other room.

"The scroll!" he gasped, abandoning his fight with her and darting into the room.

Saderia whipped around and froze, just like he had, as her gaze took in the room comfortably located just through the archway. It looked comfortable and respectful, but she could sense the power emanating from the tomb and its regality making everything pale in comparison to it. Gold sparkled from the walls, presents from Queen Tarae's closest friends and followers, and in the center of the tomb sat a sarcophagus, colorfully decorated in the shape of a tiger that looked almost identical to herself and Karenisha. Saderia let out a gasp as she realized it had been painted to look like Queen Tarae had when she had lived, and that she looked almost exactly like her. But then her gaze drifted to a pedestal that stood proudly in front of Queen Tarae's tomb, practically pulsing with power. On it sat a scroll.

Dastarius raced to the pedestal and grabbed the scroll with one paw. His eyes were gleaming with the anticipation of the power that would greet him when he recited what was on that scroll. The reality of the situation crashed over Saderia like a tidal wave and her feet were able to move again. Without thinking, she leapt for Dastarius, letting rage fill her enough to give her strength. Dastarius had no right to invade her ancestor's tomb like this and he certainly didn't deserve whatever power that scroll would give him.

She narrowed her eyes, her claws clicking on the smooth stone floor as she raced toward him. "Give me that scroll!" she shouted as she lunged at him, knocking the scroll from his paws just as some of the words became visible.

The scroll hit the ground and rolled off to one wall while Dastarius stumbled but caught himself and shoved Saderia off of him with enough force to leave her breathless. She hit the stone floor with a painful crash and let out a cry of pain, crumpling onto the floor. But she picked herself up, not letting herself get beaten so easily.

"Get out of here and maybe I'll let you live," Dastarius snarled, his eyes glinting with fury as he stalked threateningly toward her, his long claws scratching the floor.

"No way!" Saderia hissed, stalking forward with her own poorly contained anger. "This tomb belongs to my ancestor, that scroll to my family! You don't deserve to be here!"

Dastarius jumped at her at the same time that she lunged for him and they both went rolling to the floor, snarling and hissing with rage. Saderia slashed her claws across his face and felt blood soak into the fur between her claws. She glared at

Dastarius who snarled in fury and dug his claws into her side. She let out a gasp as pain flashed down her side, blood soaking into her fur and staining the floor of the tomb. She tore away from Dastarius, but then attacked him as soon as she had caught her breath, gritting her teeth against the pain. She jumped onto his back and tried to push him to the ground but he twisted and she fell to the ground where he pinned her down with one big paw, but not before she got a chance to slash his belly open.

He let out a furious, pain-filled snarl as he wrenched away from her, blood dripping from his wound. Saderia backed up a few paces so that her body was positioned in front of the scroll. "It's my duty to protect the forest," she hissed, panting. "No matter what you do, you're not getting this scroll."

His eyes narrowed, filled with hatred. "We'll see about that."

Saderia held her ground, unwilling to give up the scroll. Dastarius looked at it, then at her, and charged toward her with a ferocious snarl. Saderia tensed, waiting to intercept him. When he was close enough she jumped at him to force him away from her and the scroll, but he had a trick planned, and darted to the side, tripping her with his paw so that she crashed to the floor, slipping in the blood that had already been spilled.

Saderia squeezed her eyes shut, gritting her teeth against the pain that shot through her body as the gash in her side slammed against the hard, blood-soaked floor. But she recovered and got to her paws, springing in front of Dastarius before he could grab the scroll. Dastarius flashed his claws out to scratch her face but Saderia stopped him with her paw, claws unsheathed. Their claws crashed together, glinting in the faint light of the moon from outside. Saderia was the first to yank her paw away and duck as Dastarius's paw sailed over her head. She dug her claws into Dastarius's left leg as hard as she could until he let out a snarl of pain. His body sagged to the left as he pulled away from her.

She tried to spring at him while he was weak but he instantly intercepted her attack and slashed a gash above her eyes before she struggled free of his grasp. Her paws skidded on the floor, unbalanced by the sticky blood, and Dastarius slashed her paws out from under her so she fell to the ground. Dastarius flicked the scroll over to him with his tail but Saderia struggled to her paws, raking her claws across his shoulder and face so that he reared back.

The scroll tumbled along the floor but Saderia couldn't worry about where it went. At that moment Dastarius jumped at her, only this time she was able to sidestep the attack, though by the smallest of margins. He hit the ground hard. She jumped onto him and sunk her claws into his back but Dastarius threw her off with one powerful swing of his front leg. He pushed himself to his paws while Saderia tumbled away, leaping unsteadily to her paws, panting but ready to keep fighting if it was for the good of her forest.

"Why don't you just give up, Princess?" Dastarius snarled. "You're not going to win."

"Whether I win or not, I'm going to make sure *you* lose," Saderia retorted, taking a step backward as Dastarius paced forward.

"Poor stupid Princess," Dastarius taunted as he lunged for her. Saderia leapt out of the way but Dastarius whirled around at the same time she did and slashed open a gash in her forehead, causing her blow to falter because she was temporarily blinded by the blood dripping into her eyes. Dastarius shoved her to the ground, his claws digging into her shoulders. But Saderia rolled away from him, not knowing where she was rolling to, her vision red, but she knew she had to get away. She blinked and did everything she could to clear her vision of the blood and eventually she was able to see again. Struggling to her paws, she had just enough time to duck away before Dastarius rammed into her.

Dastarius turned and jumped at her but she dodged again, keeping low to the ground. She kicked the ground with her back legs to launch herself into the air, and ram into Dastarius, knocking him to the ground for a moment. He let out a snarl of surprise as he fell to the ground and Saderia's claws scored his face. But before she could get in any more hits, Dastarius shoved her away and leapt to his paws, still ready to keep fighting. Saderia was getting tired and she didn't know how much longer she could keep this up.

But she was determined to hold her ground. "You destroyed my family once," she snarled. "I'm not letting you do it again, and I'm not letting you destroy the whole forest this time."

"I don't think you've got the strength to stop me," he retorted.

Saderia braced herself for the next attack but at the last moment, Dastarius swerved to the left and shoved into her side, pulling her paws out from underneath her with his long claws. Unprepared for that, Saderia let out a sharp gasp as she crashed to the ground. She managed to slash her claws across his chest before she fell but then he held her down, crushing her with powerful, dark paws. His amber eyes gleamed with satisfaction as she struggled unsuccessfully to free herself from his grasp.

His eyes still gleaming with cold malice and wicked triumph, he sneered at her. "Looks like I did win, Princess." Saderia struggled but she couldn't break free. Her amber eyes widened in terror as she looked up into his face right as he lunged to sink his fangs into her throat.

She couldn't let out a scream of terror or a call for help because she was paralyzed with fear. Her mouth opened but the only thing that came out was blood as she wondered in horror if this was the end. Was this what it felt like to die? Where would she go when she was dead? Sheer terror spiked throughout her whole body, comforted only by the fact that maybe she had held off Dastarius long enough for her family to be able to stop him.

Frozen in place, she wondered if she should say goodbye in her mind, but at that moment a roar from the archway shook the entire tomb, maybe even the whole forest.

"Get away from my daughter!"

In an instant, Dastarius was yanked off of her and new life surged into her as she gasped for air and struggled to get to her paws. She heard vicious fighting and yowls of pain coming from somewhere just a few paces away. As she got to her paws and turned in that direction, she saw that Makero was fighting with Dastarius, looking so ferocious and furious, his green eyes dark and narrowed with such rage he made Dastarius look like a terrified kitten. Dastarius had no idea what had hit him and Makero roared with rage as the two animals fought fiercely.

Cia and Uncle Jash were in the archway, looking shocked and terrified, their fur fluffed up with excitement and fear as they took in the scene, looking for any way to help but frozen to the spot. Then she was on the ground and Karenisha was above her, covering her with licks and brushing her bloody fur with her soft, fluffy tail. Her eyes were wide with distress and concern, but a fiery light of furious rage danced in their amber depths.

"Are you all right?" Karenisha demanded.

Saderia blinked several times but finally she nodded. "I think so."

Karenisha breathed a sigh of relief. "We had to reopen the tomb," she whispered hoarsely. "It closed before we could follow you. We...we were afraid we'd be too late."

"It's okay," Saderia assured her. "I'm fine. I had to go through the tomb to protect the scroll, and I'm okay now. You got here just in time."

Karenisha closed her eyes and let out another relieved but shaky sigh. Then both tigers turned toward Makero and Dastarius as the fighting turned brutal and Makero, though he was fighting his heart out and fury coursed through his body, was having a hard time defeating Dastarius, who had a power-hungry, evil snarl frozen on his face. Dastarius's face contorted with hatred as he faced her father and fought with contempt and anger.

The situation returned to Saderia's still shocked mind and she quickly shook herself and turned to her mother. "I'm fine, really," she said urgently. "You go help Dad! I'll protect the scroll!"

Karenisha looked about to protest but then she looked at Makero. She turned back to Saderia with concern in her eyes.

"I'm okay," she insisted. "Trust me. I'll be fine, I promise. Right now you have to help Dad and we have to help the forest."

Karenisha hesitated then nodded with a tight smile. "I always knew you'd turn out to be like this, brave, loyal and compassionate." Then she hurled herself at Dastarius and joined Makero to help him win. Saderia watched them for a moment, concern for her parents making her feel weak with fear but at the same time ready to fight anybody in order to protect them. She saw the gleam in Karenisha and Makero's eyes as they fought bravely to protect her. For a moment Saderia was overwhelmed with the knowledge that she finally had the perfect parents she had dreamed about, the ones that cared about her so much as to risk whatever it took to protect her.

When she was sure that her parents would be all right, she turned away from the fighting and raced toward the scroll which had rolled away to rest in one of the corners by a glittering pile of gold. Trying to ignore the pricks of pain from her wounds, she sat back and picked up the scroll in one paw but let out a gasp as it opened before her, as if her touch had triggered it. The scroll was old but it felt strong in her paws and Saderia was held mesmerized by the words on it. The words were neat and graceful strokes across the old paper and they had not faded at all, even after thousands of years had passed since they were first written. As she stared at them, unable to look away, she felt power shoot into her paws and course throughout her body, as if she were pulsing with it like the scroll seemed to be. Staring at the page in awe, she read in her mind the words that said:

Heart gives an animal the power to choose right over wrong no matter how hard, and to do what is best for others, to care about those in need, earning Crown.

Crown leads to the power of responsibility, after the endurance of hardship and sorrow, the ability to make good decisions, which leads to Scepter.

Scepter leads to knowledge about the world and its creatures and courage to go out to help despite fear, choosing how to serve the forest, giving insight, seen as Eye.

Eye leads to perception and being able to see things as they are, as good or bad or something else, giving the belief that allows the world to be helped, known as Dreams.

Dreams are what must be used to help the world, to protect its animals; it is the mark of someone

who truly cares and someone who truly under-
stands, one who has a brave and caring soul and
has the capability and responsibility to handle
such a gift, one who must use this Power for good
instead of evil and protect the world and those
they care about no matter what the cost.

Saderia was awe-stricken as she read the ancient, wise words that would give an animal the Power to see the future in dreams. Something in Saderia's heart fluttered and a power greater than anything she had ever encountered seemed to light her up and spread throughout her, filling her with the strength of the ancient words. For a long time her gaze was transfixed on the old scroll, and she was unable to look away. Her mouth opened just slightly, her eyes wide with the power of the words.

But an agonized shout of pain sliced through her attention and her head jerked up to look over the scroll to where Karenisha and Makero held Dastarius down. Makero had sunk his fangs deep in Dastarius's throat and the dark lion was thrashing beneath him wildly, roaring with pain and terror. Saderia watched in horror as he turned to face her, his amber eyes filled with pain and fury. "Don't think you've won, Princess!" he snarled, "This isn't over!" But then his body went still and his head fell to the ground, his eyes glaring sightlessly at nothing.

Dastarius was dead!

Makero stepped away from the dead lion, looking grim but relieved that his life was over and he could cause no more trouble or pain. He had scratches all along his body and so did Karenisha but they weren't too horribly injured. They exchanged a triumphant glance and turned to Saderia but froze, their faces twisted with shock.

Saderia frowned in confusion as their eyes grew as big as full moons and their mouths opened in shock. She swiveled her gaze to the archway where Cia and Uncle Jash had been but now they were focused on her with the same expression, only there was a trace of fear in their blue eyes. Turning back to her mother and father, she saw confusion in their faces but also a fierce admiration, even though they were clearly baffled.

Saderia was confused as she continued to stare back at them. Why were they all looking at her like that? And there was another thing--why was it suddenly so light inside the previously black tomb? Her eyes focused on Karenisha as her mother spoke, her voice breathless with shock and admiration. "Saderia, you're...you're glowing!"

Saderia's frown deepened as more confusion swept over her, wondering what her mother could possibly mean by that. Cia and Uncle Jash were a lot more terrified than her parents and Uncle Jash exclaimed, "What's happening?!"

"What's wrong with her?" Cia cried right after him.

"Nothing's *wrong* with her," Makero murmured, as stunned as Karenisha. "In fact, I think everything's *right* with her."

Saderia continued to stare at them in confusion. "What are you talking about?" she asked, tipping her head to one side.

"You're...glowing," Karenisha whispered. "Literally, *glowing*! Look at yourself!"

Still frowning, Saderia looked down at her white chest but let out a gasp, her face twisting with shock and wonder. She really was *glowing*! A strange white light lit up her chest and her whole body sparkled with the brilliant light. Falling onto her hind legs to hold up her other paw and put it in front of her face, she gasped when she saw that it was glowing as brightly as a star at twilight. She twirled it through the air, lighting up the room wherever her paw moved. She set her paw back down and flicked her fluffy tail in front of her face, still shocked to see it emanating with that strange white light as well. The light illuminated her jet black stripes even in the darkness and made her yellow orange fur shine brilliantly. The rest of her body was shining the same way, as if she were made of hundreds of specks of light.

"What's going on?" she breathed, her eyes wide with wonder but not terror. She noticed that her fur was no longer bloody from the battle and the wounds had closed up, not ruining the beautiful glow coming off of her. She realized with a start that it felt like she was glowing on the inside, as well. Strength flowed through her body along with a tingling warmth and happiness, leaving no place for negative emotions like fear or anger.

Karenisha, Makero, Cia and Uncle Jash all stood speechless, staring at her in awe and wonder, although love and warmth lit up her parents' eyes, along with pride. Saderia could only stare back at them wide-eyed and open-mouthed but then her attention was drawn back to the scroll and she let out a gasp when she realized that the words had changed. The words were different, still written in that beautiful, neat handwriting that had once belonged to Queen Tarae, but now they were shining as brightly as Saderia. This time Saderia read the words out loud without even consciously deciding to do so.

The daughter of the fiftieth generation of the royal family will be gifted with the Power of Dreams stronger than any member of the royal family before her. Her spirit will light the way to a bright, marvelous future. Her soul will guide her through her destined path, and will help lost souls find themselves again. She will be expected to handle her Power responsibly and wisely, and do what she believes is best. The hardships she will face will give her strength. She will go on to do many great things, and Heart, Crown, Scepter, Eye and Dreams will help and guide her.

Slowly Saderia looked up from the writing to face her family, her fur still glowing with a beautiful, magical light. "I'm..." she whispered, but she trailed off, unable to say the words. She couldn't believe this was happening; it wasn't possible. There was nothing special about her! Sure, she tried to do the right thing, she listened to her instinct and she might even have strange dreams, but she didn't think she was anything like the scroll described. What did it mean? *How* would she go on to do great things? She didn't even want to be special, she just wanted to live a normal life with her parents.

But Karenisha was gazing at her with such pride and admiration that tears spilled over her cheeks. "*You* are the daughter of the fiftieth generation, Saderia." She beamed at her daughter, happiness emanating from her almost as brightly as Saderia's glow. "I always knew you were special, and so wonderful."

Saderia shook her head in horror. "But I'm not special!" she exclaimed. "I'm not any of that, and I can't see myself doing all the things it said! I can't be the one this is talking about!"

"You can't deny a prophecy," Cia murmured, her face lighting up like Karenisha's. She and Uncle Jash were no longer afraid and just as marveled as her parents were.

"A prophecy?!" Saderia exclaimed. "No, that can't be what this is! I...!"

"Saderia, stop doubting yourself," Makero told her gently. "Nobody, yourself included, can deny all the amazing things you've done and how you've kept going."

"But I..."

"Your modesty just makes you even more special," Uncle Jash teased warmly.

Saderia blinked. "Modesty?! It's not that, I just...!"

"Makero's right, and you can't deny how amazing, how special and wonderful you are," Karenisha whispered, more tears spilling over her cheeks with pride and awe.

"The glowing proves that," Makero added with a warm grin.

Saderia just stared at them, shocked, and her attention was drawn back to the scroll where the words still shimmered brightly. As she stared at the words, the scroll trembled in her paws and Karenisha's words floated over to her.

"Just believe in yourself," she murmured. "You can do a lot more than you think, and you're a lot stronger and braver than you believe."

Saderia looked up from the scroll, her paws still shaking as she gripped it, but then she smiled at her family. The powerful feeling surged through her now that she was accepting it and her body tingled with excitement. She was still afraid and confused about why a 'prophecy' had chosen her, and she didn't know how she could ever live up to its expectations, but as long as she had her family and as long as she kept going and trying her best, maybe she could come close to living up to the insightful words. Maybe she could live out her dreams.

Chapter Thirteen

Together

Several weeks later, Saderia was living the life she had always dreamed about. Her fur had lost the glow it had had in the tomb but she still felt as though she were glowing whenever she woke up and found her parents waiting for her in the dining room. It had been very hectic after that night in the tomb, and everything was a blur afterwards. A lot of explaining was needed, but it all got done and now they were all free to live their lives.

The forest had been stunned when the animals had learned that Karenisha and Makero were back from the dead. That night, they had dragged Dastarius's body out of the tomb and buried him, letting everyone know that he was dead after they told the whole forest at a meeting what he had done and where the King and Queen had been for so long.

But there were some things that the forest never got to know, like the fact that the prophecy had appeared to Saderia and made her start glowing. That was something they decided to keep to themselves, Saderia especially. She didn't want the whole forest looking at her any differently than they already did, with awe and wonder in their eyes, like she was some kind of freak.

Another thing they kept to themselves was

what happened to the scroll afterward. It had been debated fiercely for a long time that night whether they should destroy the scroll or not because of the trouble it might cause if it managed to get into the wrong paws again. But eventually they decided they couldn't destroy the precious scroll, especially after the prophecy it had presented to Saderia. Instead they resealed the tomb and each promised that they would never tell anybody the way to get inside it.

Saderia tried to forget about the enormous expectations and Power placed on her shoulders, and most of the time it was easy. Karenisha and Makero treated her no differently than they would have treated her even if she hadn't been glowing because of a strange, thousand-year-old prophecy. Cia and Uncle Jash were more wary at first but eventually they acted more normally, and they even loosened up a bit.

Saderia now had a voice and she used that voice to make her dreams come true. Her room was quickly remodeled the way she wanted it to be. Now the walls were blue, as was the carpet, and her bed was exchanged for a more comfortable, casual cerulean blue one, without a canopy but with a comfy pillow, blanket and mattress, things she hadn't thought existed before. The vanity in her room was disposed of and she never had to wear accessories ever again. From then on, she called the shots and she was able to be whoever she wanted to be.

Her room was filled with a desk in the vanity's place and a closet was constructed where she could put sports stuff and things she treasured inside. Saderia kept her bedside table and inside it kept her mother's diary, a book, and pieces of paper as always. But she chastised herself, knowing she didn't need to call it her mother's diary anymore; instead she could call it *her* diary now.

She was allowed outside whenever she wanted to explore in the forest, or play outside and she was free to get dirty and dusty, along with other freedoms she hadn't been exposed to. Karenisha and Makero played with and spoke to her every day. Saderia was once again amazed at how perfectly they lived up to what she had imagined. Not a day would go by when she and Karenisha wouldn't challenge each other to a tree climbing contest or a race through the woods. Makero would of course join in and so would Cia and Uncle Jash sometimes. Saderia made every day count in case she didn't have a tomorrow with them.

Karenisha and Makero became King and Queen much to the delight of the forest. Cia and Uncle Jash were no longer the rulers, but they still helped them with the decision-making and were recognized as equally important animals. Because of their support and the King and Queen's return, the royal parties were no longer needed which was a good thing, because it would only bring back bad memories for Saderia.

The animals were all happy that Karenisha and Makero were back because they were truly great leaders, as Saderia and everyone else soon saw. The animals who Saderia had helped get their children back were eternally grateful. Another thing that Karenisha and Makero made sure the animals were clear on was that Saderia wasn't just some Princess figure, that she had a personality and wanted to be treated like a normal animal with thoughts and feelings like anyone else. Saderia was grateful for that and it reflected just how much her parents knew her, despite their short relationship. And the animals did treat her a lot differently, as if she were normal and someone they could relate to, not someone they had to bow to.

Karenisha and Makero also fixed Saderia's schooling. Soon, she would attend normal public school to learn like a normal animal and make friends and do all the things she had dreamed of doing. Her tutors were no longer needed and Cia and Uncle Jash recognized her intelligence almost as quickly as her parents once she had a chance to show her true self.

Karenisha and Makero still looked at the forest around them as if it were more precious than gold. Her parents had been locked away for a long time, and it was difficult but wonderful for them to adjust to life in the forest once again, where they had the freedom they had always dreamed of having when confined within the walls of Dastarius's dungeon.

They still stepped out every morning to watch the sun rise as if it were a miracle happening, the same way they looked at Saderia sometimes. For a while, Saderia had shown them around and given them a tour of their old home when they had gotten back. Now she took them through the forest and told them the names of trees, bushes and berries and took them into town to name all the shops and familiarize them with their forest again. Eventually they got the hang of it and were able to go through their forest just fine, but they kept Saderia with them anyway. As they grew more accustomed to living freely in the beautiful, natural world they tried to act normal but Saderia knew it would be a long time before the song of a bird, the sun warming their fur and the softness of grass beneath their paws would be anything short of a miracle to them.

Cia and Uncle Jash, more open-minded now, apologized to Saderia and they agreed to start over. They approved of all the things Karenisha and Makero had set up to give Saderia more freedom. They treated her like she would have wanted to be treated and even played with her outside where Cia could get her fur dirty! Saderia respected them for doing their best to take care of her and even more for admitting their mistakes and having the courage to start over. She was sorry she had ever doubted them, and made sure they would have a much better relationship in the future.

Karenisha and Makero gave her Princess training, but it was the kind she would have wanted. They gave her situations that made her think, situations that hurt but would teach her. They taught her how to make decisions, no matter how tough, although, in the events that had taken place with Dastarius, she had already learned that. But they let her help out with royal situations presented to them and even though it was hard sometimes, Saderia appreciated that she got her chance to speak her mind and take care of her forest.

Saderia's life was almost utterly perfect, and not because she was royalty, but because she had a family that cared about her and that she cared about just as much. It wasn't because she got what she wanted but because she actually had a voice and a choice. But although her life was like a miracle now, she still wondered about the things that had happened to her, starting with when she had first had the dream about the fire, a dream she now credited to the Power that was passed down in her royal family.

She still had nightmares about Dastarius, not the ones that felt real enough to come true--the ones the Power gifted her with--but normal, yet equally frightening nightmares. She dreamed about the dungeon, about fighting with Dastarius, running away and leaving her parents behind and always woke up sweating and gasping. Her parents had nightmares, too, which was why she didn't bother them with hers; it would just worry them.

She often thought about how anyone could possibly be like Dastarius and she thought about how lucky she had been to find her parents and even help them. But when she wasn't thinking about things like that and her nightmares, she was wondering who it was that had helped her in the dungeon and who had written her that note that had led her to the missing children. She conceded that some mysteries would remain mysteries forever, but she was still curious.

And she still had the prophecy on the scroll hanging over her head. She still didn't know how she would live up to those expectations or why the scroll had picked her out as special, but she had to accept it. And she knew she could face it, too.

She could face anything, as long as she had her family. Her family of five.

Sarah Renée has loved writing from an early age. She has been writing short stories since the age of four and at the age of ten, she came up with the idea for The Tiger Princess, writing the novel when she was twelve. She is fascinated with wild animals and the wild world outside her home, and has an obvious great love of tigers. She enjoys spending time with her cats, reading, drawing and playing her violin when she is not writing. In her free time, she is constantly daydreaming about her many characters, creating new ones, and coming up with interesting adventure story ideas. She is thirteen years old.

12325247R00216

Made in the USA
Lexington, KY
05 December 2011